30 Failures BY AGE 30

Katharine!

Published by
Katharine Miller/Sparkling Observationalist Books
sparklingobservationalist.com

ISBN: 9781449587420

Miller, Katharine, 1979-
 30 Failures by Age 30/ Katharine Miller.

Dedicated to my mother, who inspired me despite
all her best efforts. She gave me the strength
and humour to deal with the absurdities of life.

contents

Foreword
Introduction

Failure 1 - Successfully drive a car   13
Failure 2 - Develop an ample bosom   15
Failure 3 - Maintain the art of conversation   18
Failure 4 - Ride a bike   20
Failure 5 - Failing to procreate   22
Failure 6 - Stick to a fitness regimen   24
Failure 7 - Join a religion   27
Failure 8 - Keep a best friend   30
Failure 9 - Participate in public nudity   32
Failure 10 - Join team sports   34

Things to know by age 30   37

Failure 11 - Attend overnight camp   39
Failure 12 - Exercise patience   42
Failure 13 - Move to NYC   44
Failure 14 - Obtain a healthy glow   46
Failure 15 - Master nice penmanship   48
Failure 16 - Learn/speak a second language   51
Failure 17 - Develop a drug addiction   53
Failure 18 - Ride a roller coaster   55
Failure 19 - Stay in hospital   57
Failure 20 - Win a prestigious award   60

Things to do by age 30   63

Failure 21 - Run afoul of the law 65
Failure 22 - Hold full-time employment 68
Failure 23 - Contract chicken pox/measles 70
Failure 24 - Get married 72
Failure 25 - Visit a strip club 74
Failure 26 - Defend myself 76
Failure 27 - Own property 80
Failure 28 - Perform in public 82
Failure 29 - Leave North America 85
Failure 30 - Be truly selfless 87

A list of even more failures 89
How to be a failure 91

Failure Bingo card 93

About Katharine! 95

foreword

In 2009, my 30th birthday as rapidly approaching and I decided to take stock of my life to that point. Had I achieved everything I'd wanted? Did I meet all the expectations of society? Does it matter?

On reflection, both in 2009 and the following years, I can say that I have achieved most of the goals I set for myself in the innocent, pre-Internet days of youth. Admittedly, these are small scale achievements that will impress no one but my eventual biographer.
If there's one lesson to be learned from the 1967 film *Bedazzled*, it's that one should be as specific as possible in one's wishes. (The lesson to learn from the 2000 film *Bedazzled* is that Brendan Fraser is no Dudley Moore.)
Now comfortably over 30, I continue to defy all of society's expectations and it doesn't really seem to matter. Failing to meet societal expectations has not made me less of a human being. I continue to set new goals and fail or succeed them on a daily basis.

This slightly expanded edition of *30 Failures By Age 30* now offers more lists of failures and as well as proper lists of things you should know and do before turning 30. If you are over 30, fret not! This book is still relevant to you!

—Katharine!
February 2016

introduction

Once upon a time, 30 was old. It was Grown Up. It was almost middle-aged. If you weren't married by age 30, something was wrong with you. If you didn't have children, something was wrong with you. If you weren't settled down with life all figured out, you'd screwed up somewhere along the way. Or so it seemed.

Turning 30 isn't as big a deal as it was once. Thirty-somethings can't be old because then the forty-somethings have to admit that they're old and the fifty-somethings must grapple with the possibility of being completely irrelevant. Many thirty-somethings I know aren't married and haven't had children. None of us seem to have life figured out.

Reaching any sort of milestone in life feels more important than it actually is. And so, in honour of my 30th birthday, I scribbled out a list of 30 things I'd failed to accomplish in this sizable chunk of life.

The 30 Failures list is not one of light-hearted or thrill-seeking experiences, like kissing a foreign ambassador or bungee jumping. Every item on my list represents a path not taken and any one of these failures could have had a dramatic impact on the outcome of my life. This is what happens when you defy expectations. Whether by chance or by choice, by not doing these things, I became, and remain, a social misfit.

This is not *1,000 Things To Do Before You Die*. This is not *Eat, Pray, Love*. The end of this book will not reveal some greater truth or meaning of life. Or maybe you can find it, if you dig deep enough into the subtext. But I make no promises. I can't guarantee any heart-warming or feel-good moments. I can guarantee a few chuckles at my expense.

FAILURE #1
successfully drive a car

Thinking back on my early life, I don't recall ever possessing a real desire to drive. I wasn't constantly daydreaming about all the places I'd go in my car. I did sort of expect that I would join the wheeled masses. Driving is just one of those skills that people assume everyone has—like the ability to tie a shoe or use the toilet. You just do it and don't think about it.

The interest I developed as a teenager arose mostly out of peer pressure and envy. And, if we're honest, to get a teensy taste of freedom that driving might allow. Didn't I want to join the kids in the parking lot who were sitting on car hoods and smoking questionable substances? Didn't I want to cruise the main strip in my small town? Well...The call of the open road came from an unlisted number, so I didn't pick up.

My father received the call of the road early in his life and spent most of his life as a mechanic and cross-country truck driver. He dedicated so much time to his vocation that it actually led to his demise. While out on a call with his towing service, he was struck down by a drunk driver. My father was also seduced away from my mother and they had been apart for most of my young life. I was 14 at the time of his death and had very little contact with him. Tragic all the way around, but less painful than you might expect from such a loss. My father's death, and to a lesser extent his career, did have some impact on my decision to resist driving. In my explanations to strangers bewildered by my license-free existence, I have given his death more credit than it actually deserves. I missed out on sitting on my daddy's lap and helping him steer his semi cab. He didn't give me a rusty old clunker that I could bang into a couple of lampposts. But through his death, I was afforded other opportunities. Had my parental units made different decisions and life gone a different way, I might be compiling a list of 30 different failures.

My mother didn't drive—or own a car—until her late 20s. My sister was 30 with a newborn when she finally got her license. My maternal grandmother relied on the kindness of strangers and relatives to ferry her around town. My maternal great-grandmother would hire a taxi to visit the liquor store and deliver her booze order to her door. So, it wasn't entirely expected that I would jump behind the wheel on my 16th birthday. However, out of obligation I took driver's ed and through youthful optimism I bought a car.

My most memorable driving experience involves the test drive of my green 1996 Dodge Neon. Whoever had the bright idea to put an unlicensed 16-year-old in the driver's seat of a brand new car and take it off the lot should've been fired that day. My mother and I took it out into the neighbourhood behind the dealership. I tried to make as many right hand turns as possible as I hadn't quite mastered the art of steering and right turns were easier than left turns. Returning to the lot, I was so focused on trying to park the car between the lines of the space that I drove up onto the sidewalk, managing to stop mere inches from the showroom entrance. We bought the car I would call Raymond a few weeks later, probably from a different dealership, but I couldn't get motivated to take him out for a spin.

The number of times I've operated a vehicle is far outranked by the number of boyfriends I've had. I struggled to find a co-pilot who could be kind and patient and non-judgmental as I fiddled with all the dashboard doodads. Eventually I gave up, content with the notion of being a life-long passenger. The Volkwagen ad was right—there are passengers and there are drivers. And I call shotgun.

I gave up my car long ago. For all the freedom driving supposedly gives you, I think I have just a bit more. I'm free of insurance premiums and maintenance costs. I don't worry about my car getting stolen or damaged. I am not on the quest of the perfect parking space. On road trips I am the designated navigator and snack dispenser. The rising cost of gasoline has no direct impact on my pocketbook. Since moving out of rural Alabama, I've chosen locations based on walkability and public transit. My general rule is if a destination unreachable by bus or by foot, it's not my destiny to visit. This is probably a smarter way to live now, what with efforts to be eco-friendly and reducing the carbon footprint or whatever planet-saving buzzword you're using these days. Maybe I'm not a failure but a genius, way ahead of my time. Uh-huh.

FAILURE #2

develop an ample bosom

In general, flat-chested girls are often ridiculed and overlooked as sex objects. We don't get fair representation in the media. The best role models we have are Olive Oyl and Helen Gurley Brown—neither great examples of female empowerment. In fact, most small-breasted women involved in the media have succumbed to insecurity/pressure and undergone breast augmentation. Even Helen Gurley Brown went up a cup size at age 73. We don't have charming euphemisms for our breasts—unless you consider "mosquito bites" to be a term of endearment. More often than not, we are made to feel ashamed of our bodies. Granted, it's rare to find anyone who actually has a positive body image. It seems like everyone's got some flaw they're looking to conceal or change.

Through exposure to television, magazines, billboards, and a well-endowed older sister, I assumed an ample bosom was the norm. I fully expected that by my 13th birthday I would develop my own set of perky breasts that would magically lift me out of my pudgy awkward childhood. Sadly, I remained pudgy and awkward for another six years. And by age 30, I think it's safe to assume that I'm not just a late bloomer.

We're programmed to expect some sort of development in the chest region. And when it doesn't quite happen, it's very disappointing. Waking up every day with small breasts is like Christmas morning and discovering all your friends got Barbie dream houses and you got a package of socks. Well, I suppose those might come in handy. Anyway, it's a bummer. Not only personally, but to suitors and beaus. When a boy realizes that he's fallen for a small-chested girl, he has to quickly disguise his disappointment. "Oh...well that's alright...y'know, more than a mouthful is a waste..." he says, followed by a half-hearted chuckle. And even though both parties move past it and might settle into a cozy little relationship, the ghost of his disappointment lingers.

Despite my lack of buoyancy, I have dated pretty steadily since my first official date as a freshman in high school. Being small-chested hasn't rendered me a hopeless spinster, never to know the feel of a man's touch. However, even though all of the guys have been kind and accepting, none have been especially enthusiastic on first encounter of my A-cups. In other words, no one's said "Oh boy, I love small tits! This is the best day ever!" And in some cases there might have been some expectations that I might be willing to do certain other things. Y'know, since he'd been so gracious about accepting me as I am. We don't keep in touch.

All of my friends, growing up and through adulthood, have been substantially more endowed than myself. I couldn't related to any of the issues my friends had with their breasts. Problems with staring, underwire, bra snapping, back problems, and accidentally dropping spare change into cleavage were foreign to me. So I had no one to join me in my quest for the perfect bra or to try any of the silly regimens offered to small-breasted suckers. All of the experimentations were done sequestered in my bedroom, away from prying eyes and derisive comments.

There are a variety of devices a girl can use if she's dissatisfied with the size of her chest—exercises, cremes, makeup tricks, falsies, and so on. Thankfully, I grew up with alternatives that were more sophisticated than the ol' stuff the bra with socks or tissue method. Over time, I tried the Wonderbra, the water bra, the bra with gel-filled cups, and those inserts that look like chicken cutlets. Some more comfortable than others but none could authentically mimic the real things and it all felt deceptive. Any attention received while wearing the falsies wasn't honest. And it was never fully appreciated. If any padding felt unsecured, I would spend the evening checking myself out in every reflective surface and one eye on my pretend cleavage just in case anything shifted. This distraction made simple activities like talking, eating, and breathing quite challenging. And forget about bowling!

I'll admit that thoughts of augmentation have flittered through my mind. I never gave it serious consideration because I don't see the long-term benefits and if I was going to splurge on physical alterations, I'd probably have lasik or cyborg modifications. Of course, then I'd be a flat-chested lady cyborg, further disenchanting the hordes of geeky boys in my target demographic.

More than feeling inferior or lacking femininity, I feel gypped. I feel like I was robbed of fun and exciting social experiences. People actually look me in the eyes. None of my friends' brothers "accidentally" walked in on me in the shower. I didn't attend hair band concerts or Mardi Gras parades and lift my top. I was never a Girl Gone Wild. My dreams of entering the adult entertainment industry were crushed. No. I had to be funny. And creative. And good at Boggle.

Maybe I could dedicate the next 30 years of my life to small breast advocacy. Promote myself as a successful member of the ibtc. That would first require a success. Maybe I'll toss out all the padded bras and embrace my body as it is, not as society perceives it should be. Or maybe I'll write a novelty book of euphemisms for small breasts.

FAILURE #3

master the art of conversation

Can you tell me when being a polite, quiet person fell out of vogue? At what age should one be heard as well as seen? When is it appropriate to speak even when not spoken to? I think I was absent the day this stuff was covered.

When I was younger, my quiet nature was a virtue. The adults in my life were so impressed with my ability to sit down and shut up. The teachers appreciated how well-behaved I was and often stuck me with the task of taking down the names of all the heathens who would cause a ruckus when no adults were present. Sometime after graduation, though, people began to equate quiet with weird. A few would ask "Why are you so quiet?" in an accusatory tone, as if politely listening to a conversation was a sin.

As an introvert and recluse-in-training, I have little occasion to practice the art of conversation. In my defense, I can blame some of my social awkwardness on my hearing impairment. To avoid the frustrations and (quite literal) headaches that come with trying to concentrate on multiple strains of conversation, I just stay out of social situations as much as possible.

When I am thrust into social settings, conversations generally fall into two categories: things I've never done but others have and things I don't care about. So when someone starts off by saying "One time I was so wasted..." or "Remember at Bible camp when..." I know it's time for me to sit back and think about foods I have enjoyed because I won't have anything intelligent or fun to contribute to the conversation.

Since my silence was encouraged when I was a kid, I never got properly socialized. Where does one go to learn small talk? I went to public school. My family only ate around the dinner table on holidays. Church? Oh, it has to be church. I didn't really go to church, so that must be the source of small talk refinement. Anyone can talk about Jesus!

"So, how about that Jesus?"

"Yep, he's a swell guy."

"Some weather we've been having."

"You know who enjoyed a good rain shower? Jesus."

Sometimes I surprise myself and carry on delightful conversations with one or two people. Most of the time, however, I am a frog in a shoebox (*Hello my baby, hello my honey...ribbit*). And content to sit back and let people talk at me or just let the surrounding conversations wash over me, absorbing the bits and snippets of chatter that filter through my faulty ears. In fact, there are times when I don't notice that I haven't been actively participating and I don't feel awkward about it. But then some wisenheimer pipes up with "Jeez Katharine, stop hogging the conversation...maybe next time you'll let someone else talk." Reminding me once again of my social inadequacy.

As a writer, I have control over how and when I share information. In a conversation, the other party can ask questions about things I'd rather not discuss—like family life, occupation and why I moved from the Deep South to the Great White North. While writing these essays, I can present sensitive information and touchy topics far better than I can articulate them over cocktails in a bar. On the rare occasion that I do get into a conversation and someone asks those seemingly banal getting-to-know-you questions, I freeze up like a deer in headlights. I don't have easy responses because I haven't had an easy life. "Where are you from?" usually leads to "Why don't you have an accent?" And I just don't want to get into a discussion about my hearing impairment with someone I've just met and will possibly never speak to again.

I can get away with the ol' nod-and-smile for just so long before people catch on that I'm not as polite as I am socially dysfunctional. Maybe I'll sign up for Remedial Small Talk for Introverts at the learning centre. I should strive to become more engaged and engaging. At the very least, I could add more guttural utterances when someone asks me about the weather.

FAILURE #4
ride a bicycle

Wheels are not my friends. They do wonderful things for other people and provide numerous helpful services. But we do not get along. Oh, we've tried to make it work, but I just kept getting hurt.

Every attempt to go roller skating led to me collapsed on top of one twisted ankle or another. A trip around the go-kart track ended with tears, an injured foot and a missing shoe. My elementary school had piles of old tires as playground equipment and I was always falling into them. I even stub my toe when pushing a grocery cart.

And so I've never ridden a bicycle. Never experienced the freedom of taking off on my bike to ride with friends down cheery tree-lined suburban streets. Never rode a tandem bike with a beau around a riverfront park. Never entertained fantasies of competing in the *Tour de France*. Never had a legitimate excuse for wearing spandex shorts in public...

Like anything worth doing, riding a bike requires time, practice and patience. No one in my household had experience in bike riding. The only bicycle we owned was a stationary exercise bike in my mother's bedroom. I would occasionally play on it while watching *Perfect Strangers* on TGIF. Because my feet couldn't reach the pedals, playing really meant honking the horn at Balki and Cousin Larry until my sister would yell for me to quit it. Unlike a car or pony or personal chauffeur, we probably could've afforded a cheap, used, beat up old bike for me to crash into a tree. Living just below the poverty line in the U.S. did mean that we couldn't afford the hospital bills if I'd crashed myself into a tree. And I wasn't the most graceful child. Even with three seasons of dance classes, I was pudgy and clumsy. I could bruise simply by sitting down.

But looking back, I didn't yearn after that little pink bicycle with the tassles and the basket with flower decals. It was never on my Christmas wish list. Instead, I dreamed of a limousine with a hot tub in the back after I saw it in the Phil Collins' video for "Take Me Home". Surely I couldn't get hurt in that! When my family moved to the outskirts of a smaller, more rural town, bike riding became even less of a possibility. Living right off a highway meant the streets weren't really child-friendly. Or pedestrian-friendly. Unless you liked trying to cheat death by dodging log trucks.

I suppose it's not too late to learn. I could go into a local bike shop and buy some cheap, beat up old thing—plus all the silly safety accessories that one needs these days. After suffering through a hilarious montage of bike accidents, I could be feeling the wind in my hair and bugs in my teeth. And, finally, I would have an excuse to wear that spandex bodysuit.

FAILURE #5
failing to procreate

This is not a failure.
I do not consider my abstention from parenthood itself a failure. It is simply one more example of how choices I have made set me apart from the norm and make socialization a challenge. The decision to remain child-free is still an unpopular one in North America, but my womb is delighted to not be contributing to the world's population and overcrowded public school classrooms.

That I emerged from rural Alabama without becoming a young mother is a miracle as the penises of young virile Alabama boys are strongly averse to condoms. I don't know if this is a religious matter or an issue with extra foreskin or the lack of proper sex education in schools. I knew several girls who got knocked up before graduation. Some girls arrived at high school freshman orientation with their newborns. Which seems like an awful lot of work just to get out of writing the "What I Did on Summer Vacation" essay.

I don't have any gut-wrenching experiences with abortion, miscarriages or pregnancy scares. As miraculous as it may seem, I have reached the end of my 20s without purchasing a home pregnancy test. And yet I am not a 30-year-old virgin. Is this a sign of practiced responsibility or undetected infertility?

Over the years I've heard the arguments for and against motherhood. I took it all under advisement and arrived at the logical conclusion that I would not be a mommy. In a society that believes an empty womb is a wasted womb, motherhood is an assumed eventuality. Advances in science and modern medicine still leave me prey to older women patting me on the knee and telling me it's not too late to change my mind and have a little one of my own. A friend of my mother once told me that pregnancy increased breast size, as if the prospect of larger breasts would convince me to have children. Um, no. Also, what an odd thing to tell a 16-year-old-girl.

Breeders like to accuse non-breeders of being selfish, claiming that we don't understand the struggles and rewards that come with being a parent. But we do understand the investment of time and money. We see the sacrifices good parents have to make in order to give their children better lives than they themselves might've had. We see the mothers on the street loaded up like pack mules just to take one child to the park. We are aware of what it takes to be a good parent and we're opting out of parenthood altogether.

If I am selfish, though, isn't that a good enough reason not to procreate? Isn't it just as selfish to bring a child into this world simply because you want one? "Go forth and multiply" is an antiquated notion. But I recognize that it's not my place to dictate whether other people should or should not become parents. All I can do is hope that those who have chosen parenthood did so for the right reasons and hope that they'll respect my decision.

Being child-free by choice means missing out on more social events. If I'd had a child, that would've opened up opportunities to re-experience childhood, if only vicariously. Just think of all the toys and events and activities I missed out on that I could share with this new creature! However, I'm not thrilled with the idea of having a kid just so it can do all the things I didn't get to do. "Look here sonny, you're going to Welding for Toddlers whether you like it or not."

Our neighbourhood, once full of aging Polish immigrants, is filling up with young families. Women who might be closer in age are still worlds apart. There is a noticeable social chasm between me and the 20- and 30-something mothers. I cannot relate to child-rearing anecdotes. I can't contribute to discussions about the latest in baby technology. And no, I'm not particularly interested in looking at photos of babies smeared with food substances.

The price for freedom is loneliness. I am free to pursue endeavors that I couldn't with a papoose strapped to my back. My boyfriend and I do what we want, when we want without worry of lining up a sitter or obligatory play dates. If I should find myself alone and getting on in years without someone to take care of me, I could adopt a sullen teenager for companionship. Maybe in 20 years, the topic of rejecting motherhood won't be as taboo as it is today; that the breeders and non-breeders can live in harmony without admonishing the other for their lifestyle choice. Until then, I will continue my streak of not peeing on sticks and to sidestep the strollers on the street.

FAILURE #6
stick to a fitness regimen

I like ice cream. I also like muffins, cupcakes, bubble tea, chili cheese fries, pizza, bread pudding, oatmeal raisin cookies, and any combination of pasta and sauces. And you know what? Those things do taste as good as being thin feels.

The problem is that I like to eat but I do not like exercise. This is because I am lazy. If presented with the option of playing frolf (frisbee golf) in the park or watching a marathon of *Welcome Back, Kotter*, I'm probably going to choose the Sweathogs over actual sweat. Lounging on the couch while watching things I've seen ten times before is more appealing to me than going out in the fresh air and sunshine. And at the end of the day, I don't smell like grass and outdoors. I probably smell like Cheetos.

And so it is that I reached my 30th birthday out of shape and still wrestling with body issues. With no reunion, wedding or bikini demanding a toned body, I lack the motivation to get into shape. I've been battling the bulge most of my life and have tried different exercise programs over the years but none of the routines stick. This can be partly blamed on my laziness but also on my intentions for different workouts.

As a child with various allergies and maladies, I wasn't encouraged to run around or participate in physical activities that might result in severe injuries. I was mostly instructed to sit down and be quiet. I began life as a roly-poly baby and carried around my baby fat for the first 17 years of my life. Then I just got grown-up fat, which isn't nearly as cute or endearing. With my own food budget and a craving for sugar, butter and lard, I consumed a lot of fast food during my teen years. By age 19 I hit my heaviest at 175 pounds. By today's obesity standards, 175 is nothing. Why, it's almost average. But it is still big enough to mean you have to shop in the husky ladies' department.

Once I moved from my hometown to a booming metropolis, there was less and less of me to love. I was walking instead of being driven around. I was no longer making trips to Taco Bell or KFC for my daily dose of the tasty trinity. Such a dramatic lifestyle change meant the weight dropped off. By my 20th birthday I was down to 115 pounds. The loss alarmed my mother, who was probably convinced I'd taken up drugs and other unsavory habits in the big city.

Over the past ten years I've put a little more Kraft Dinner on my bones but I haven't come close to becoming Fatharine again.

I still walk everywhere but I just can't get into exercise. Some exercises involve special equipment or heavy machinery. Others involve counting. Videos require watching people in better shape than myself pretend to have a better time than me while perspiring. All fitness programs demand a certain level of enthusiasm for physical activity. "Oh boy, let's jump up and down 20 times! Woo! Now let's see how close we can get our knees to our eye sockets! Yay!" I don't even express that kind of enthusiasm for things I love. What I need is an workout program designed for lazy cynics.

When you're a recluse-in-training like myself, it can be very difficult to meet new people. Bars and clubs can be too noisy to make social connections while libraries are too quiet. Apart from jobs and church, most social settings require some sort of routine consumerism. Gyms involve routine consumerism with the added bonus of physical improvement. Except nowadays people exist in their own bubbles, shutting themselves off from outside distractions through their portable electronic device of choice.

In my pursuit of physical fitness as social activity, I joined a "walking group" once that turned out to be me and two larger single women engaging in early morning bitch sessions about the opposite sex and the perils of online dating. I had to quit because 6:30 am is too early for me to be defending my relationship to bitter 30-something ladies who believe all men over 45 are slimy creeps.

Just before the Big Move to Canada, I enrolled in a ballet class which was filled with 60-year-old fangirls of the tightly packaged teacher-boy. The acoustics in the classroom were lousy and all the ladies wanted to be close to the soft-spoken danseur. I quit after two or three classes, after I realized I wasn't going to fit in there. A few years before that, a friend invited me to use her guest pass at Curves. I found the mix of machines and low-impact exercises accessible but quickly exhausted of the overplayed disco tunes pulsating through the tinny speakers. If I never hear "YMCA" or "Hot Stuff" again, I'll pen a personally handwritten thank you note to Jesus.

And so, the quest for washboard abs remains a solo endeavor. Occasionally I'll have one muffin too many and discover an unwanted muffin top. Then I pull out the Pilates book and the yoga mat and try to muster up the will to lose enough so I can once again comfortably wear pants without elastic. But exercise at home feels like a chore. Though I know the 15-minute walk (uphill both ways and, for five months of the year, in snow) to and from my subway station isn't much, it's more active than simply getting in and out of a car.

That I've been able to escape obesity for this long without strict diet and fitness regimens is an amazing feat. It will no doubt catch up to me. As my metabolism slows to match my sloth-like movement, I suspect I'll be forced to go up a pant-size or two. But maybe I'll stumble on the perfect workout program or a gym for cynical, socially awkward nerds. Or I'll invent a Wii game that combines Boggle and *Dance Dance Revolution*. In the meantime, there's a very special episode of *Welcome Back, Kotter* I've never seen.

FAILURE #7
join organized religion

> "Personally, I don't have the talent to believe."
> —Arthur Miller, *The Atheism Tapes*

I am a godless heathen. I have not be seduced by any one deity.
I have not been programmed for the kind of fanciful thinking that most
religions require. As a mere observer of organized religion, it's very easy
to dismiss them all as lunacy. But this isn't about the rejection or dismissal
of all religions. I don't begrudge the believers for their beliefs. If your religion
motivates you to stick to the moral high road and helps you make sense of this
realm, then pray on, brother. This is simply a reflection on my experiences
in faith-based matters.

Technically, I was born into the second-most widely ridiculed religion
on the planet. My parents were a couple of (supposedly) devout Jehovah's
Witnesses. They were dragged along when their mothers had been seduced
by the promise of impending Armageddon and righteous immortality on Earth.
If you're only familiar with Jehovah's Witnesses from hilarious stand-up
comedy routines or tidy boys leaving copies of the *Watchtower* on your doorstep,
you don't know the half of it, buddy. Here's what I know:
they convince their members that the outside world is doomed. Witnesses
are forbidden from celebrating holidays or birthdays. Forget Santa Claus and
the Easter Bunny, kids. Witnesses refuse to vote or participate in any act
of national patriotism. They are encouraged to limit socializing with
non-Witnesses. If they manage to remain morally superior to everyone else,
when the current world order has been destroyed, the righteous will achieve
physical immortality on this planet, which will morph into a global Garden of Eden.

By divine providence, I was spared from participating in their special brand
of crazy. After my mother's second divorce (not entirely by her choice), she/we
were disfellowshipped (shunned!) and did not return. Thereabouts, she lost her
faith. You might have a crisis of faith as well if you lost your one true love, were
rejected by those who you thought were your friends, unceremoniously
excommunicated from church and your own mother treated you like dirt

in public settings, all while working a crap job to straddle the poverty line with two children to support. Her sacrifice prevented me from further ridicule. Can you imagine if I'd been a pudgy, bosom-less, bespectacled, hearing-impaired girl and a Jehovah's Witness?!

So I was raised without faith. Without faith, it's difficult to accept—and be accepted into—organized religion.

When I was 16, I did attend a few church sessions with my boyfriend at the time. The Southern Baptist services were solemn and without much ceremony, alternating between standing and singing and listening to some guy yammer about the moral issue of the day. The girls in Sunday school were excited that Easter was approaching which meant chocolate (!!!). The pastor took his family to Disney World for spring break amidst the Southern Baptist boycott of the company and its parks. They all seemed quite content to leave me be on the outskirts, rather than embrace a potential new member of Team Jesus.

I don't discount the social values of organized religion and the routine of attending church. If anything, I might give it too much credit. Organized religion provides community and social activities that one might not get from public school or cable television. Could my social life have been improved by a couple of church-sponsored bowling trips? Perhaps. But I don't think gutter balls and rented shoes and soda pop with the youth pastor would've renewed my faith in a higher power. My bowling score might be a little better, though.

In my thirty years, I have yet to experience a religious awakening. I didn't have it when my father died. I didn't when my sister laid in a hospital bed for several weeks with severe blood clots after giving birth. Based on those school assembly lectures from former druggies/ex-cons/crack whores who found Jesus in a dingy motel bathroom, one gets religious when one has hit their lowest point. I obviously haven't hit my lowest point yet. Or maybe Jesus should find nicer places to hang out. Panera Bread has free wi-fi. The food court at the mall has some questionable characters who could probably use a hug from Jesus.

Since abandoning the Bible Belt for a pair of atheist garters, I haven't encountered much in the way of religious pressure. Most people tend to be tolerant of other's religious practices though I've learned to not discuss religion with strangers. Telling people I don't attend church prompts the follow-up question, "Well, what would you be if you did go to church?" They don't respond favorably when I say, "A unicorn."

If this was a Hollywood movie, the act of writing this essay would've taken me on a spiritual journey and it would end with me having found faith in a lovable deity. This is not a movie and I remain a faithless cynic. Don't pray for me just yet. I haven't fared so terribly as a non-believer. Despite what I might feel in my darkest moments, my most basic needs (and a number of frivolous whims) are fulfilled. Aside from a couple of missteps during a turbulent stretch of puberty and a few adult indulgences, my moral gps and common sense have kept me out of dingy motel bathrooms. Maybe there is some Heavenly reward for living a pious life. Maybe I'm cheating myself out of my own Heavenly reward by not subscribing to a brand of worship. Right now I'm content to celebrate the birthdays of my loved ones, participate in patriotic hoopla for two countries and just enjoy mortality.

FAILURE #8

keep a best friend

If I had only one regret in life, it's that I didn't have that steadfast bosom friend, that one person to turn to when things got rough. Where was the Anne to my Diana? The Mame to my Vera? The Denny Crane to my Alan Shore? I mean, I wasn't totally friendless. I just never got my best friend. Well, not one I could keep.

In the early years, my mother arranged play dates for me. Unfortunately, the pickings were slim amongst the morally superior set and my "friends" were limited to a girl whose mother dressed as the Icee polar bear, a girl named after a soft drink brand, and a boy. None of them shared my enthusiasm in staging stuffed animal vaudeville revues. Neither did they want to know how dreamy I found Peter Scolari and whether he was dreamier in *Bosom Buddies* or *Newhart*.

By the time I'd entered grade school, I'd lost my morally superior pals. And it seemed like everyone was already paired up. I did fall in with a few other chubby awkward girls. In my grade school's speech therapy sessions, I bonded with the spiky-haired boy from Illinois and the girl with the lisp. But one friendship never truly prevailed over all others and my friends each had someone else to confide their deepest desires and secrets.

Occasionally one friendship would become more predominant over others. Phone calls with this one person would increase in frequency and length. We'd sit closer at the lunch table. Then the tides would turn and I would lose favour with this person. Because my friends lived in different neighbourhoods and my mother couldn't get out of her bed most weekends, the majority of my friendships ran their courses over the phone and through notes passed in school hallways. There was no one in my 'hood that I could trust to tell me that leggings were not pants and that, although I might blare Billy Joel and TMBG from my stereo, the oversized black t-shirts indicated hardcore headbanger. My BFFs and I weren't having sleepovers, trading clothes and experimenting with whatever teenage girlfriends experiment with. The girls I knew weren't terribly interested in listening to the Shelley Berman album I found in my mother's closet. They mostly wanted me to eavesdrop on their conversations with the boys they liked.

My most treasured friendships were ones with boys. This is because these boys were able to think about things outside themselves. The girls could really only think about boys. Sure, they could talk about movies and television…as long as there was an attractive boy involved—either on screen or in the room with us. Admittedly, I was guilty of thinking about boys myself. Of course the "boys" I thought about were unattainable and not really boys so much as grown men. I was always closer to my boyfriends than my girl friends. The boyfriends were willing to endure Shelley Berman. Still, no one was willing to discuss the geeky dreaminess of '80s era Peter Scolari.

Without a lifelong BFF, I have been able to go through permutations and reinventions with minimal criticism. No one's been there to remind me of my Bad Decision Dinosaur moments. No one to whom I could confide my own deepest desires. No wind beneath my wings.

If I were on the path to become a better person, I would contact my former BFFs to find out why our friendships fizzled. I suspect that we're all better off as Facebook acquaintances, with the ability to leave comments on freshly uploaded photos without the messy drama of everyday life. No one really wants to dredge up old heartbreaks and failures…unless they're writing a blog about old heartbreaks and failures.

As I get older, it gets more difficult to find kindred spirits in a 10-mile radius. My closest friends reside miles away, across several borders, which makes meeting for bubble tea and giggling nigh impossible. These days my partner serves double-duty as lover and best friend, which some might look on as a great thing. But I feel bad that he has to endure my gripes along with my gropes. Thankfully he's very tolerant of my silliness and ideas involving finger puppets and burlesque shows.

I haven't given up on the possibility of finding a proper BFF. *Boston Legal* has given me hope that I'll find my bosom flamingo. Until he (or she) comes along and invites me for balcony visits and sleepovers, I will endeavor to tend to existing friendships, foist my silliness on them once again and maybe remind them—and myself—why we bonded in the first place.

FAILURE #9

participate in public nudity

When I think back on my youth, I don't recall any invitations or occasions for public nudity. In general, public nudity tends to be frowned upon, though I suspect for the wrong reasons. Failing to bare more than teeth in public isn't so much of a failure in itself—it's the lack of bravery to even consider doing it. Bawk ba gawk.

And I don't think I'm alone in my reluctance to drop trou amongst strangers. You might be struggling to think of instances in which public nudity would be appropriate. Has Emily Post ever covered this sort of thing? Certainly Miss Manners laid down some etiquette for skinny dipping!

I've never gone skinny dipping down at the quarry. My hometown probably didn't have a quarry. But there might have been some swimmin' hole where the youths would strip and frolic 'neath the moonlight. My invitation must've gotten lost in the mail. Perhaps none of my young beaus needed to resort to such trickery to get me unclothed. (Miss Manners had a chapter on that, too, right?)

Streaking is another act of public indecency that I haven't had the occasion to perform. But then, I'm not prone to any bouts of athleticism. Which is also why you'll never see me at one of those clothing-optional bike rides or at the Co-ed Naked Jai Alai tournament.

I will also confess that I haven't exhibited any signs of exhibitionism. I have never, on purpose, participated in flashing, mooning or anasyrma. If I owned a classic trench coat, I might entertain notions of traipsing about town in only my London Fog and bowler hat. But not in winter. Or on Thursdays.

Now those are just the deviant deeds. We haven't even considered the legally acceptable forms of social nudity—the nude beaches, nudist colonies and naturist clubs. Just the word "nude" conjures up grand fantasies of airbrushed bathing beauties and hard-bodies. In theory, these places could be great locales to toss off your trousers and your inhibitions. That is, if you're willing to have your dreams shattered by the lumpy bottoms of reality.

For whatever reasons—body issues, fear of skin cancer, lack of bravery—I'm not quite ready to shed my threads for all the world to see. But, who knows?

Someone might decide small breasts are high art and want to paint my portrait for public viewing. Maybe I'll get involved with a local burlesque show. Or maybe I'll take a road trip where I moon my way across the TransCanada highway. In the meantime, I'm going to look for an Emily Post's *Guide to Nude Etiquette* on Amazon.com.

FAILURE #10

join team sports

Some people may be born athletes. Others may be pushed into athletics by over-achieving parents vicariously pursuing latent Olympic dreams. The rest of us are left to fumble and flail about in various playing fields to measure our own athletic aptitude. I discovered, through nature and nurture, that I am not an athlete.

My elusion of sports-like activity stems from a combination of lack of opportunity and disinterest. This makes my failure list for physical and social reasons. Thankfully, despite women's lib and athletic equality between genders, being a girl who doesn't play sports doesn't hold the same social stigma as it did for boys. I'm no less of a woman because I didn't have a catch with my mom. But maybe I could've fared better in a social realm if I hadn't feigned sustained injury to get out of playing volleyball in junior high.

There are a few things you should know about the wee Katharine. When I was seven years old, we discovered three important things:

1. I needed glasses.
2. I couldn't hear very well.
3. I was allergic to insect bites/stings.

As a result, we also learned:

4. Children are insensitive little bastards.
5. I am a crybaby.

I invite you to reach back into your own childhood psyche, to imagine that you are six or seven years old, everything's kind of a blur, sounds a little bit muffled. Then imagine 20 kids shouting and taunting, with some sort of vaguely round-ish object hurtling towards your face. You might shed a couple of tears of frustration yourself.

My newly discovered physical handicaps were enough to convince my mother that I should be indoors at all times. The public school system rarely agreed with her. And in lower Alabama, the weather doesn't much warrant much indoor play. However, after a few convincing notes from my doctor, thePhys. Ed. coach gave me an exemption from kick ball. In grades four through six, the school found indoor activities to occupy me with during the outdoor sessions of P.E. But the earlier years scarred me just enough, thank you.

My one official experience in being on a team comes from my grade school. It had a school-wide mandatory program that split each class into two teams: the Green team and the Gold team. I was on the Gold team. Every spring, the school would hold a festival where the teams played different games, did some sort of a relay race, and other activities which I have blocked from my memory. I think of my five years at the school, the Gold team won once. Which led to the next lesson:

6. I am a sore loser.

During school hours, we didn't have many opportunities for team sports. When it was kick ball season, one half of the class would be pitted against the other half to battle it out for half an hour. Sometimes other kids would show up to school in various sporting jerseys, advertising their upcoming game against some other pee-wee league team. Only then would I feel a twinge of envy, that someone belonged to something that I didn't. I felt the same way about the Girl Scouts. Did I really want to wear a uniform? No one ever asked and I just assumed these were secret clubs. For all I knew, getting into girl's softball was like trying to join the Freemasons.

Eventually puberty and laziness set in and I couldn't be motivated to do anything but watch cable television and listen to my Billy Joel tapes. Most sports took place outdoors and I still wasn't allowed to play outside. Indoor sports at school were limited to basketball, volleyball and the occasional roller skating excursion. If I am not an athlete, you'd be correct in assuming that I am not an athletic supporter. The closest I've come to being a cheerleader is making an off-colour remark while watching my high school boyfriend beat his friend at *Mortal Kombat.*

Occasionally I'll see a casual game of softball or watch a bowling league in action and ponder what it might be like to have that kind of social interaction. If I joined a team, would they be good-natured about my lack of skill and natural athleticism or roll their eyes and heave impatient sighs when I goofed up? Are there beginner level teams for people my age? Could I wear a uniform? Most importantly, could I get over the fact that I am a Sore Loser. Maybe I can find a group of disaffected 30-year-olds who hang out on the bleachers and make snarky comments instead.

things to know by age 30

1. Your own social security number (or international equivalent).
2. Your blood type and personal medical history.
3. Your parents are only human.
4. The addresses of your last seven residences.
5. All the words to your national anthem.
6. How to tip.
7. How to do your own laundry.
8. How to live within your means.
9. Basic DIY home repairs.
10. How to listen to other people.
11. Three good jokes.
12. Three life anecdotes that don't start "we were so wasted..."
13. Alcohol won't fix everything—baking soda can!
14. When you're ready to go home.
15. 30 isn't old.
16. 30 is not the new 20.
17. No one else's labels matter.
18. You don't have to justify your life choices to strangers.
19. Sometimes you have to give up on that haircut.
20. It's okay to compliment yourself.
21. No one is looking at you as closely as you look at yourself.
22. Your high school crush is not aging well...probably.
23. No one is entitled to know the details of your bedroom
    or your bank account.
24. Shortcuts rarely lead to long-term solutions.
25. Rarely are there tidy solutions for feelings.
26. Everything in moderation—except murder. Murder's just not
    a great idea ever. Unless you encounter a centipede in the shower.
    You kill that thing with fire.
27. What you're willing to compromise for someone else.
28. Small town values aren't for everyone. Neither is big city life.
    It's okay if you wind up in the suburbs.
29. Traditions are not always worth carrying on.
30. You can still do all the things, if you want to do them.

FAILURE #11
attend overnight camp

Just as television, books and movies had planted romantic notions about high school and breasts and Jesus in my head, summer camp was a glamorized unattainable fantasy. But it was not my destiny to don terry cloth shorts and frolic around the great outdoors with people who were not part of my normal world. I would not spend balmy summer evenings underneath the stars, roasting marshmallows and singing campfire songs. Instead of bunking with strangers in the woods, my youthful summers were a little different.

My earliest summers were spent with my mother's mother. I hesitate to call her "grand." She was rarely without a frosty can of PBR in her hand, with a paper towel beer cozy because that's how classy she was. Oh, and her pet name for me was "the little retarded one." My days with her were spent in her seniors residence, sitting with other little old ladies and making crepe paper flowers. In the three years I visited the old folks' home, I never saw any other children. Most likely because they were away at sleep away camp.

I spent a couple of summers in my default after school hang out— the snack bar of the Montgomery County Court House, where I alternated between reading Lewis Grizzard books and fielding questions about how I liked school, who my sister was dating and whether I was enjoying my summer. Occasionally my mother enlisted me to "help" her with her work, which mostly meant copying information from the microfiche and then looking up the parents of my classmates. I was the only nine-year-old who knew about second mortgages and tax liens. Also, I was probably the only nine-year-old reading Lewis Grizzard.

When we could afford it, I would participate in daytime summer activities. One year I was fortunate enough to indulge my creative side by taking dance lessons and a ceramics class. I squished myself into a brightly coloured leotard and learned routines to popular 1980s hits on the even days and painted tacky knickknacks on the odd days. Then I went to day camp, which compressed all the popular summer camp activities into eight hours a day. While I was involved in these programs, I actually spent time with people my age. To a normal child, it might have been a relief to hang out with youths and indulge in youth culture.

I came into it after spending years in the company of the elderly and was unaccustomed to a summer day that didn't smell like death, Vaporub and Pabst Blue Ribbon.

The trouble with any "camp" is that it implies that copious amounts of time be spent outdoors. After age seven, I wasn't encouraged to be outdoors ever. Even without my allergies, interacting with nature doesn't rank high on my list of interests. I like looking at photographs of nature. I hope that nature can hang on for a few dozen more years. But nature and I won't be playing a round of Boggle anytime soon. My idea of "roughing it" is staying at a bed and breakfast without internet access. Sleep away camp would've meant spending time in the wilderness and out of the jurisdiction of my mother. My mother and I have always had differing opinions on how far away I should be from her. She's been on the losing end ever since I outgrew the papoose. Anyway, overnight camp was never a possibility.

Those of us who attended day camp managed to accomplish most of the things kids do in overnight camp. There were brief summer crushes. The pudgy girl with the pink glasses and black elastic sports strap was ridiculed and pushed down on the playground. Unlikely friendships were forged. The pudgy girl was ridiculed in the pool for wearing inflatable floaties on her ankles. Lessons were learned about sex and gender. The pudgy girl avoided ridicule on the swing set and made up parody songs that could be viewed as morbid foreshadowing. All achieved with minimal adult supervision. At the end of the day we went home to air conditioning and television.

Do I imagine sleep away camp would have been a better experience? Given my track record with insensitive bastard children at school and day camps, it probably would've been absolute misery and I'd have called my mother to retrieve me from the hell in time for Saturday morning cartoons. After I hit puberty, my mother left me at home with cable television and bags of Cheetos and I was content to live vicariously through Hayley Mills times two and the Camp Anawanna kids of *Salute Your Shorts*.

I think summer camp provides an opportunity to reinvent yourself, a chance to try out new fashions and affectations without interference by those who've known you since diapers. The closest I got to reinvention was when I tried on my grandmother's wig and tried to learn the harmonica. Maybe if I'd gone away to camp, I would've found my life-long BFF, mismatched bunk mates turned bosom friends. Or, perhaps while on a nature hike, I could've found Jesus skinny dipping and teaching bears about love and kindness.

Oh, the failures that could have been avoided! Okay, so I can't join in when people share anecdotes about camp practical jokes or sing campfire songs. But if you want to go swinging and reminisce about microfiche and crepe paper, give me a call.

All that said, if there was an adult summer camp for people who are inept at dealing with woodsy environs, I might consider attending. They have WiFi, right?

FAILURE #12

exercise patience

If you're on line at the post office and hear someone tapping their foot and heaving sharp, dramatic sighs, it might be me. I am not a patient person. My impatience is not a quality I am particularly proud of, but it keeps me bitter. Without bitterness, I wouldn't have nearly as much to write about.

Why am I so impatient in post office queues? Why do I get restless if the subway train sits at a station for one minute too long? What compels me to dash to the checkout ahead of the elderly Chinese lady? I have Places to Be and Things to Do, of course. Nevermind that the place is my home office and the things are wearing pajamas and looking at Apartment Therapy and Popdose online.

As often as I am impatient to get back into my pajamas, I am anxious to get out of them. I may be the only woman in Western civilization to be on time for any event. In fact, I'm usually unfashionably early. Whether it's for an interview or a casual night at the pub, I will be there 20 minutes before the scheduled time. It's a challenge to look cool while sitting in a waiting room or bar all alone. And I haven't quite mastered disguising my ire when I'm left waiting 20 minutes past schedule. Especially without WiFi, so that I can make passive aggressive comments on Twitter and Facebook.

But really, how'd I get this way? I suppose I am a product of modern society. Like many of my generation (and a few before), I've been spoiled by our fast food culture. I expect my whims to be met instantaneously. I want what I want when I want it and I don't want to wait for it. Haven't you heard? We live in a fast-paced world where everyone is busy. We don't have time to wait for slow-cooked meals. We don't have time to sit through three minutes of commercials. I'm Entitled. Gimme!

In my chosen profession, I have been conditioned to work at breakneck speed on short deadlines. Generally I'm able to do so without breaking much of anything, not even a sweat. Commercial creativity, though, is a hurry-up-and-wait vocation. Hurry up and write that article or design that ad and send it off to the client for feedback. Clients always want to receive the creative content immediately, like yesterday. Minutes turn into hours and hours turn into days before a client will respond to creative work. Oftentimes the client will respond mere hours before a project goes to press with loads of suggestions and changes. If only an accredited post-secondary institution offered Wizardry and Time Travel degree programs.

Impatience can be a virtue if it's properly harnessed. In 2009, I took on the challenge to take some old essays and shape them into book form. I started the project in February. The book was print-ready by June. Now it's available online and in stores in Toronto. If I'd gone the traditional route, I'd still be waiting for rejection letters to trickle in. Now I can get rejected directly by consumers!

By nature I am restless and fidgety. I am not content unless I'm chipping away at some fancy plan. I like to get things done. Some people work for accolades or applause, but I've got a jones for that sense of accomplishment. Unfortunately, the accomplishment high wears off pretty fast and my mind wanders onward to the next project. Sometimes, when the restless demons need to be quieted, I'll visit the local swing set or turn on an American International beach party movie. These distractions allow for a brief escape from obsessing over the lack of responses to my latest batch of resumés and why I'm not further along in my career. Watching a 45-year-old Harvey Lembeck as juvenile delinquent Eric Von Zipper gives me hope for the future. Perhaps one day I will be a middle-aged teenager. (It's not an entirely farfetched notion in this McWorld of ours.)

I have longed for the ability to step back, take a deep breath and say "que sera sera." Let life happen instead of trying to control the uncontrollable. Things should run their course in their own time. My dinner doesn't always have to go from freezer to microwave in three minutes flat. I can sit through a few commercials. Some of my whims can be put off until tomorrow. Maybe the next time I get impatient behind the elderly Chinese lady at the post office, I'll invite her to join me in the park for a swing.

FAILURE #13

move to NYC

Living in a small town, it's easy to be seduced by concrete and neon.
And with a life chockful of awkwardness and misery, my mantra became
anywhere but here." For most of my life, "anywhere" was New York City.

I know, the whole move-from-rural-Alabama-to-sophisticated-NYC is such
a cliché. Which may be how the notion got lodged in my brain in the first place.
Well, and the *Arthur* movies. Eventually I wised up and gave up the dream o
f living in a tiny roach-infested rathole and suffering for my art. I set my sights
on slightly smaller cities.

My decision to not move to nyc was made in part thanks to the decade-
plus battle I had with my mother titled "No, that's too far away... why don't you
just move back home?" which usually resulted in my remaining in the
Southeastern quadrant of the U.S. Though my mother has lost at this point,
the battle goes on, silently.

To be fair, I did give my mother false hope from the outset. I moved back
home after my first semester at university when my roommate,
a Bible-thumping perky blonde girl annoyed me with her fear of black people
(and you're attending a predominantly African American school, why?) and
insinuations that my late nights were a result of frequent fornication sessions
with my boyfriend when I was really getting bleary-eyed and cranky at ridiculously
long theatre rehearsals.

When I turned 19, I quit university and moved to Atlanta. Living in Atlanta
quenched that thirst of big city life. My father had lived there when he was my
age. But here's the thing—it's not what you'd call pedestrian-friendly. To me,
Atlanta is the Southern perception of what big cities must be like. The drivers
are crazy impatient and there's a cacophony of horns on the city streets.
I quickly grew disenchanted with the city and its multi-storey escalators.
While trying to decide on my next destination, my mother and I locked horns
and I wound up moving in with a different boyfriend. In retrospect, moving
in with a boy I'd only known for mere weeks was not the smartest move
romantically. But it was a successful move in the ongoing NTTFA... battle.
It sent the message that I would rather deal with unpleasant BoyDrama and

mentally disturbed felines than move back to the cozy bosom of Home.
To do that would be to admit failure!

Of course, when the inevitable end came to my tumultuous affair, my family
was so willing to jump to my aid and help me move anywhere I desired, given that
it was far away from That Boy. My mother lived in Orlando in the '60s with my
sister's father. We vacationed in the area frequently. My mother spoke often of
moving to nearby Ocala. We hauled my stuff from Northern Georgia down to
Central Florida. I did not expect the backlash I got several months later, as she
became increasingly bitter over my decision to live where she vacationed.

After six years in Orlando, it was time to pull up roots and relocate.
Eventually my family stopped vacationing where I lived. Opportunities were
drying up. And so we set our sights on points North. I don't want to delve too
much into the Big Move, so I'll simply say that some stuff happened, people did
some things, and now I live in Toronto. The decision to move here wasn't
impulsive. And, if you think about it, it's not all that surprising. See, Toronto
is like that friend you like but never really thought of in "that way." While NYC
is the hunk that everybody wants—including you. In the end, you realize that
friend has everything you were looking for and was right there the entire time.
After watching tons of movies set in nyc and finding that they were actually
filmed in Toronto, I found that I'd been lusting after Hogtown my whole youth.

I was able to visit NYC in 2004. We were sidetracked by a hurricane that
wouldn't let us get home, so we stayed with friends in the city. After having
spent a week living it up in Toronto and Montreal, I was tired and cranky and
in no mood to be wooed by the city I'd dreamed of for so long. It failed to charm
me and I was secretly comparing it to my new love. I should give it a second
chance sometime. Maybe I could phone up my old college roommate and
we could meet at the Empire State Building.

Would my life be different if I'd refused to compromise and moved to NYC?
Sometimes it's fun to ponder the what-ifs. But after I've pondered, I'm content
to hop on the TTC and visit all those places I saw in the movies. "Anywhere
but here" may still be my mantra, but the meaning is a little different these days.

FAILURE #14:
obtain a healthy glow

Look, as a Caucasian, I cannot possibly relate to the struggles and discrimination and violence encountered by other races. The physical and emotional oppression of an entire race of people makes my getting picked up by the ears by a freakishly tall bully in grade school look like petty griping. But I do know how it feels to be judged by one's skin colour.

I never had any of my basic freedoms stripped away based on the colour of my skin. I was only made to feel uncomfortable within it. And even then, only by insensitive bastard Caucasian children. Insensitive bastard children know no boundaries in the crude art of ridicule. Actually, ridicule is a tad harsh in this instance. We'll call it criticism. As someone involved in commercial creativity, I am open to honest feedback and constructive criticism. And, my position on procreation aside, I'll grant that sometimes those darndest things out of the mouths of wide-eyed babes can be amusing. I still have no idea how to react when someone exclaims, "You're so white!" at me. Similarly, I struggle with crafting a clever response to "But you look so young!" Are these insults? Compliments? Insults wrapped in compliments and dipped in jealousy? I can tell you that my youthful appearance and skin tone are direct results from staying out of the sun and wearing my sunglasses more than Anna Wintour.

During my tweenage years, the occasional bitchy beige girl took the opportunity to ask snidely, "Why aren't you tan?" and "Don't you ever go outside?" They were being rhetorical. They didn't care. They just needed to make me aware that they were judging me just as harshly as I might've been judging myself. If I responded with, "Is that rhetorical?" The girls would snort about my use of a big word and go compare tan lines with her toasted friends.

As I got older I would encounter people—heavily made-up middle-aged women, mostly—who went into rapture over my "gorgeous porcelain skin." "Oh, she's just like a little doll!" they would exclaim to my mother. Of course they were meeting me under the flattering fluorescence of mall lighting. People at the beach or at poolside were less enchanted with my blindingly flawless complexion. They were just blinded.

I don't have to tell you how I achieved my Ultra 00 (according to the Merle Norman make-up packaging) skin tone. The 60-watt incandescent bulbs that lit my childhood homes don't have the same impact on skin colour that the UV rays of good ol' American sunshine does.

I was the pigment-challenged sheep of the family. My father had a mechanic's tan. Years of being in the sun and doing manual labor had turned his fingernails black and his skin a nice burnt sienna. My mother told me I would call him "my fat brown daddy." He did not accept this term of endearment warmly, I was also told. My sister spent the bulk of her late teens through early thirties in pursuit of the perfect tan. She split her free time between tanning beds and sunbathing by the pool. I dedicated my free time to watching *Kids in the Hall* marathons in bed and bathing in Cheetos dust. Her skin would glow like a lightly glazed golden Thanksgiving turkey. Um, well, my fingers were orange.

I would be lying if I said I was always content with being near translucent. While I haven't followed in my sister's tan lines to the tanning beds, I have experimented with tan-in-a-tube. Um, well, my fingers were orange. My legs never changed beyond a milky white. It's the closest I've ever come to believing in God's will.

Since escaping the Deep South, no one in my new life wastes a thought on my skin colour. Canadians are not bothered if your skin is lighter than beige. With nearly five months of winter each year, there's little motivation to run around in the good ol' Canadian sunshine.

South of the border, my skin tone still elicits polarized reactions.Sometimes I get a compliment. Occasionally someone feels compelled to ask if I'm a goth chick. But being paleface doesn't have the same stigma from 15–20 years ago. Thanks to skin cancer and science, it's actually fashionable to forego the extra pigment. My peers are no longer concerned with my outdoor activities. I take pride in never worrying about tan lines. I can wear as many or as few straps as I'd like, though the latter might lead to public indecency charges.

FAILURE #15

master nice penmanship

No child has ever been as excited to learn how to write than I was as a wee tot. By the time I arrived at school, I was burning to write down all those stories I'd been composing in my head over the prior six years. There were stories about detectives and teenage pregnancies and depressed elves to be written!

By age three, I was speed reading those Dr. Seuss books and comprehending a fair amount of the TV Guide. My mother began teaching me how to draw letterforms. In the back room of the Kingdom Hall, she'd draw dots on a small pad of paper and I'd connect them to form letters. While my peers were in kindergarten, taking naps and eating glue, I was at home watching *Gidget*, practicing writing my name and learning about lazy dogs and the quick foxes who jump over them.

Having proved to my mother that I could sing all the songs from Sesame Street and draw realistic spiders on my bedroom wall, we agreed it was time for me to enroll in public school. I skipped kindergarten and went straight into first grade, where we were taught the Zaner-Bloser style of printing. So, excited—and feeling a little bit cocky with the two years of practice I'd had—I put pencil to elementary writing tablet and began combining circles and lines to make letters. I don't think anything made me happier in my early childhood education than the language arts subjects. I excelled in writing and spelling. And my newfound ability to manipulate language provided an escape into fantasy worlds of my own making. The letterforms weren't elegant but they were legible and easily distinguishable from one another. Life was grand.

In third grade we moved on to cursive writing. In theory, cursive handwriting is flowy and elegant and inspires grand romantic notions. T he D'Nealian cursive is none of those things, especially when formed by the hand of a gawky eight-year old. Suddenly the letterforms looked different, felt different. This is not how I wanted my letters to look. But I scribbled along, hoping one day to be allowed to pursue a classier handwriting style. Armed with the basics of penmanship, my classmates and I started tinkering with the letterforms. Pulling inspiration from older siblings and fonts from magazine ads, we played with shapes and sizes. The boys tried writing as small as they could. The girls took liberties with dots and line weight. My lowercase a's went from one-storey to two-storey and back to one-storey again. Then I discovered my n's and r's were too similar and began setting my R's in small caps amidst my lowercase letters. My cursive style morphed into something altogether different. My letters became narrow and started blending together. Hello individuality, goodbye legibility.

Soon after the start of junior high, I got my hands on my mother's electric typewriter. The quality of my penmanship diminished. When I bought my first word processor, I hardly wrote anything in longhand anymore...Yes, a word processor—that dandy piece of technology that bridged the gap between typewriter and computer. And much like other interim technology—eight-track and laserdisc players and zip drives, the word processor has faded from consumer memory. I'll admit, if it weren't for my dependency on the Internet, I'd still be using my 1993 Brother word processor.

My dream of having elegant penmanship was short-lived. I had Ideas and Thoughts of Great Importance that needed to be jotted down immediately. I couldn't get bogged down with swoops and flourishes and perfectly centered dots. My mother and sister have attractive, legible, feminine penmanship. To read one of their notes, you can tell that care was taken to form each letter. They make the extra effort for neatness and clarity. My handwriting has devolved into messiness. It's barely legible and straddles the gender divide as I quickly scratch out my thoughts before they dissipate.

Despite my dependency on the electronic formation of letters, I have great appreciation for the art of penmanship. Handwriting is a truly individual method of expression. It's personal and human, an intimate form of communication. The way a person handles a pen can indicate mood and personality better than any emoticon. I am saddened by the imminent extinction of penmanship. As schools start encouraging kids to master qwerty before they learn the ABC's, we might see the handwriting limited to fine artists and hipsters. Typographers of the future may dedicate themselves to the creation of fonts that mimic great examples of penmanship from the 20th century and earlier.

Could I take on the challenge of retraining my hand and develop a nicer handwriting style? Should I download worksheets of the different styles of manuscript and cursive printing and start over?

It sounds like a nice exercise, not only for handwriting but also in patience. Maybe I could develop a system of handwriting based on popular typefaces or a course that teaches elementary level printing and the fundamentals of typography. Think of how much better the pizzeria signs will be in the future!

FAILURE #16
learn/speak a second language

I like learning. I like words. It wouldn't be too far-fetched a notion that
I might like learning words in a different language. And yet it hasn't happened.
My unilingual status could be attributed to laziness. Or my impatience.
We could even pin my lack of language alternatives on my lack of practiced
religion. Had my mother relapsed into Catholicism, I might've been forced
to recite pious prose and maybe picked up a little Latin.

I have a mixed relationship with the spoken word. With visual and hearing
impairments from the outset, the early years of my life are a blurry, mumbling
mess. Bless Gutenberg and his press for making literature accessible.
The printed word made it possible for me to pretend to understand the spoken
word. If I'd had to rely on *Hooked on Phonics*, you wouldn't be reading this essay.
So. Yes. I think we can all agree that, over the course of my 30 years, I have
mastered and conquered the English language. What about those other
languages then?

Please understand, I do not believe that everyone should speak English
or "American" as some might in the Western world. I appreciate the rhythms
and melodies of other languages. As I walk through the cultural mosaic of this
melting pot of a town, I encounter dozens of dialects from one block to another.
I've no clue what they're saying, but it's beautiful.

For the past 14 years or so, I've been flirting with French. My high school
gave us two options: French and Spanish. In retrospect, I believe the deciding
factors for kids—myself included—were field trips, cuisine, and teacher
(one was a hard-ass, the other relinquished power of her classroom to videos
of popular movies with French connections, but not *The French Connection*).
Being a fan of pastries and foreign language films (the one genre where
subtitles are generally accepted in mixed hearing society), I chose French.
Despite acing the course, I was unable to piece together a logical sentence
en Français post-graduation. Oh wait, here's one: *voulez-vous coucher avec moi,
ce soir?* Oh, teenagers! What won't they say?

Without the incentive of passing marks, I do find it difficult to muster the
motivation to pick up a new patois. To pursue any secondary or tertiary

language seems to be an academic feat—learning for the sake of knowledge rather than practical use. I do like knowing things, though. And the actual pursuit of knowledge wouldn't be terribly hard, what with the magic of the Internet, iPod applications and books. Retention and proficiency, there's the tricky bit. Proficiency demands practice. Retention requires rigorous repetition. Who's got the attention span for that?!

Now that I live in a bilingual country, I will eventually give into my sense of duty and become more acquainted with French. Casual perusals of cereal box labels will turn into late night sessions memorizing dictionaries and diacritical marks. French and I may become best pals, but I'll never know any language as intimately as English. Of course, it's entirely possible that we'll all be speaking in Esperanto within the decade, rendering all romantic languages unnecessary.

FAILURE #17
develop a drug addiction

In an alternate reality, I have inherited my mama's trailer and inhabit it with several illegitimate babies from multiple donors and my ill-conceived lover *du jour*. The first spawn would've been obtained at some point in my high school career or shortly thereafter. This life would be made bearable with some form of chemical escape or a nicotine habit which also allows me to keep up my novelty lighter collection.

Alas, I have no novelty lighter collection. There is nary a lighter in my possession. My mother's trailer is occupied by new owners—faceless strangers with mysterious backgrounds and questionable morals. And I have reached my 30s (mostly) drug-free, thanks to one defining moment in my early teens.

My exposure to drugs as a youth was very limited. Like, maybe I saw a few episodes of Miami Vice and that "very special episode" of *Gimme a Break*. Aside from what I've seen in movies, I am incredibly naive about drug culture. I have no idea how much recreational drugs cost. I wouldn't know what to ask for…do dealers have printed menus of their offerings? I suppose not. Also, is it customary to tip your dealer? If so, what percentage? I would be laughed out of the opium den, for sure.

As I entered my formative teenage years, my mother and I moved into a trailer park on the very outskirts of a very small town. Fortunately, this particular park was mostly clean and populated with family types. If deals were being done, they were conducted in the wee hours and away from impressionable sorts like myself. Still, in civilized society, trailer living is equated with white trash and it's amazing that I have been able to distance myself from that stereotype.

The closest I have gotten to any drug use was during my freshman year of high school. My BFF of the year dragged me out to the designated smoking area for a chat about BoyDrama and a nicotine fix. Someone offered me a cigarette and I agreed. In my defense, I was 14, my father just died and I was coping with that along with the typical teenage woes. The BFF lit the cigarette —a Marlboro Light, maybe. It was foul. The taste offended all of my taste buds. My mouth is accustomed to the sweet and savory. This was worse than

accidentally getting gasoline in your mouth. I'm not sure I was invited back
to the smokers' corner. Certainly I wasn't invited out to the edge of the parking
lot, where the real shit was happening...probably.

I'm sure my taste in romantic companions played a role in my drug-free
existence. While my mother fretted over the day I'd bring home that tattooed
prison-bound Romeo on a Harley, I was hanging out in the science wing and
swooning over the Poindexters. If those guys had pot, they were Bogartin' it for
their anime marathons.

I have been offered marijuana fewer than half a dozen times. I have rejected
every offer. Why? Shouldn't I have tried just once, for "research purposes"?
Was I afraid of germ-laden spliffs offered up by guys with iffy hygiene?
Or terrified that I'd do it wrong? Had all of those anti-drug assemblies in school
been effective in more than just getting me out of math class?

Honestly, the whole drug culture does not appeal to me. I am unable
to rationalize how ingesting foreign substances by otherwise unnatural means
to achieve a brief mental escape from reality. That's what television was
invented for, right? Well, and the promotion of needless consumerism. The only
foreign object I've put up my nose was a pencil eraser. In my defense, I was two
and my imaginary friend just died. I did not inhale. Well, not so much did not
as could not.

This is not to say I'm a total goody-goody without vices. I enjoy an adult
beverage on occasion. Were it not for the help of caffeine, I would sleep 17 hours
a day instead of the usual 10 hours I get normally. As I get older and deal with
chronic pains and aches, I am reaching for more OTC medications. The sciatic
nerve pinch serves as a constant reminder that I'm no longer a sprightly youth.

Would drug use have had an impact on my social life?
Could I have been a social recreational user? Or would I get hooked on the
harder stuff that results in lots of time holed up in the bathroom alone? I don't
know. I might have a deeper appreciation for black light posters. I do know that
I am so far removed from the drug world that I was unable to intelligently
discuss any of the harder substances for this essay. The amount of research
I would have to do just to make cracks about cocaine or...see, I can't even come
up with a second thing, is daunting. I'm better off sticking to things I do know,
like bubble tea and the merits of Art Frahm's paintings. I may revisit the whole
topic when someone creates a dealer menu that can only be read in black light
or by the flame of a limited edition sterling silver Daffy Duck lighter.

FAILURE #18

ride a roller coaster

Your incredulity over my failure to ride a proper roller coaster is not without merit. I've had countless opportunities. My boyfriend was a member of the American Coaster Enthusiasts (which is not, as you might first imagine, an organization against condensation rings on the coffee table). I lived mere steps from an amusement park with a giant roller coaster. I can offer only one solid reason for my failure: I am a weenie.

By nature, I am not a thrill seeker. Given the option of bungee jumping (remember when people did that? Good times.) or watching *Bill & Ted's Bogus Journey* on cable, I'm going to pick the dumb movie on cable every time. But then, even the mundane things can give me pause. Escalators, for example. Until I was 16 I had no idea that escalators could terrify me. Then I met the one in the CNN building—steep, multi-storied, and chock-a-block full of people. So steep you couldn't see the top. And the handrail was out of sync with the steps, so my arm kept creeping up to my neighbour in front of me. I would later learn that Atlanta is full of long, steep escalators. This is not a fact they advertise on their postcards.

I am not afraid of heights. I have an irrational fear of being some distance above ground and then being dropped from that distance. I love playground swings but even then, I don't want to get swinging too high. And, of course, if I do relent and go on a Ferris wheel or gondola, the other people in my party like to make me squirm by rocking our vehicle as if to show me that we're in a sturdy piece of machinery and we're not going to plummet to our deaths on a silly amusement park ride. This method of reassurance might have worked some 20-odd years ago, but we're living in a different time, where things are not well made and people don't take as much pride in their work. I'm not saying all roller coasters are shoddily made or unkempt. I'm saying you don't need to be a jerk in the face of someone's fear, however convoluted and irrational.

As a kid, I went with various groups of people to the state fair. My participation at the state fair was limited to playing carnival games and eating carnival food. No ride—except for a couple of dinky "baby" rides—and no scary things. In those days, I was also forbidden to eat hard candy or popcorn for fear that I'd choke (or actually enjoy childhood). Irrational fears are hereditary, apparently. The fair is a magical place—bright lights illuminating the normally vacant fairgrounds, the air thick with cheap cigarette smoke and manure. It's a place where even your dreams can be deep fried! Who needs a roller coaster when there are caged monkeys demanding you roll grapes down their pvc pipes? Wait...I'm not sure the state fair had a roller coaster.

"But Katharine," I hear you saying, "you lived in Orlando for six years. How could you resist the siren song of the many roller coasters surrounding you?" Just lucky, I guess. Well, luck and my discovery of another irrational intolerance—theme park lines. Bless the brave souls who can stand around in the Florida heat in former swampland amongst other sweaty souls of varying girth and odors. Godspeed to the ones willing to withstand whiny brats and their cranky parents, oblivious teenagers, and bitter Florida residents. If you can survive two hours of all that, you deserve much more than seven minutes of a cheesy amusement park ride.

I understand the appeal of riding a roller coaster—the anticipation as you creak up the hill quickly followed by the exhilaration of whooshing down the other side, the wind pulling at your face as you fwish around the corners and thwipp down another quick hill. I've seen those first person pov videos. The whole experience looks a bit cathartic. A former theme park employee friend of mine would often ride a coaster at the end of his shift so he could scream out the frustrations of the day. Imagine a whole train full of people riding the Rock 'N' Roller Coaster just to release tension, shrieking and screaming away the stress and anxiety of life. That's kind of poetic. And kind of creepy. But also kind of apt for the kind of mass-individualized culture we live in these days. I prefer my stress and anxiety to be gently prodded away by the hands of a skilled masseur.

It is doubtful that I will ever find the courage to ride a coaster, to feel the wind in my eyes (drying out my contact lenses) and hair (not my own) in my mouth. I do work everyday to overcome my apprehension on escalators —I've stopped bursting into tears whenever a heavyset person is in front of me. And, if you promise not to be a jerk and rock the car, I might go on the Ferris wheel with you. I'll buy the deep fried cotton candy.

FAILURE #19

stay in hospital

A man goes to the doctor and says, "Doctor, I broke my arm in three places." The doctor says, "Stop going to those places."

Failures can be tricky. Sometimes there are successes lurking within the failures. Ever the pessimist, I am still willing to present success in the form of failure. It's less "braggy" that way. Many people will find stories of my sheltered childhood to be sad and pitiful, if not vaguely amusing. On the positive side, none of these stories end with my going to the hospital. Thanks to paranoia and borderline poverty, I have entered my 30s with bones unbroken and all of my original parts in near mint condition. All right... "gently used" condition. My life has never been threatened by illness or injuries. Although I'm sure certain people have wished me physical harm at some point.

Make no mistake, I was not a healthy child. I've had strep throat so many times that I probably hacked out my tonsils during a coughing fit. With two of my major senses dulled, I lacked the grace and poise necessary for those child beauty pageants my sister always wanted to enter with me. It was those leg bruises and my aversion to frilly dresses that kept me from being the next Morgan Brittany. (And totally not the fact that my mother pre-emptively cut my hair so that my father wouldn't kidnap me and try to pass me off as a boy... but I digress.) My most common childhood ailment was insect stings. We discovered by chance that I possessed the power of severe allergic reactions to a common fire ant bite. And in my day, adults were still prone to tossing children outdoors under the guise of allowing us to partake of that fresh air and sunshine" while they sipped martinis and told dirty doctor jokes. Inevitably, I would get bitten. And, inevitably, some wise-crackin' adult would insinuate that I sought out the fire ant beds and stood in them for several hours. Let me assure you, of all my oddball childhood hobbies—and there were some doozies—taunting the stinging insects was not one of them.

Living without health insurance is living life without a safety net. I learned to exercise the utmost caution in day-to-day existence. The simplest pleasures— jumping on the bed or sucking on hard candy—were forbidden lest they lead to an expensive trip to the emergency room. So I am lacking in awesome stories of treehouse shenanigans and bicycle pileups and emergency room hijinks. And I approach every activity cautiously, weighing the dangers involved. The obvious action for me to have taken was to become more adventurous once I struck out on my own, to celebrate my independence from my mother (the original helicopter parent) by skydiving or riding a motorcycle. Admittedly, I've had a few pieces of hard candy in my adult life. Maybe I've stood on the bed. Okay, and there was that one time when I walked at a brisk pace with an X-acto knife.

I suppose it's a success that through my own self-control I have managed some semblance of self-preservation. My own idiocy has not led me into surgery—elective or otherwise. I have surrounded myself with mostly responsible people who have not put me in harm's way through their own idiocy. I have not yet had a close encounter with Death. Why do I still feel like I'm missing out on something?

I'm missing the social aspect of injury and illness. When people are telling injury stories at the bar or comparing scars, I just sit there silently contemplating whether I want to talk about infected ooze-filled ant bites with strangers or continue nodding and ummming until it's time to go home. Would anyone really be impressed that I sprained my ankle every time I tried roller skating? I have no funny albeit embarrassing stories about how I broke my arm. I had no plaster cast that the cute nerdy boy signed, which allowed us to strike up a meaningful but short-lived friendship. I haven't yet had the opportunity to bond with others over the battle—and survival—of a deadly disease.

With few family and friends, my time in hospitals as a visitor has been limited. Most people associate hospitals with disease and death. Of the five times I've been in a hospital, three were baby-related. If you're familiar with my feelings about babies, you'll understand that my perception of hospitals is also negative. But to some people hospitals are like Club Med. Those people must have good insurance coverage. My mother had a lady acquaintance who was always going to the hospital for tests and staying overnight for observation. Ninety percent of the time nothing was wrong with her. Ten percent of the time it was nothing that couldn't have been cured by "fresh air and sunshine." Or giving up her smokes and going for a walk once in a while. A popular theory was that she enjoyed the sympathy she received while in the hospital. She could rally her family to her bedside for a pap smear. Oh, if I only knew people that could be so easily manipulated! As it is, I could post a status update on Facebook announcing that I have cancer and the response would

be one "dislike" and a snarky comment like "You brought 'er, uterine cancer."
And then I'd go to the hospital for treatment and someone would try
to give me a baby.

I do have one good hospital memory from childhood. When I was three
or four I had a Fisher Price Little People hospital set. I would spend hours
playing with its elevator, clanking the plastic hospital beds together, tuning out
my sister's *General Hospital* references. This was during my "updownside" phase
where I turned all of my toys upside down and played with them that way. I put
puzzles together upside down when I was two and my mother thought
I was a genius. I turned the hospital upside down and she threw out my
application for baby Mensa.

I have no plans to cheat Death. If he beats me at Boggle, I'll be a gracious
loser. As I get older, though, it will become harder to avoid serious health issues.
Given my previous diet of heavily processed foodstuffs and mere existence
in this fantastic plastic world of ours, it might not be a matter of whether I get
cancer but which kind. My bones will crumble soon enough from osteoporosis
thanks to 30 years of carbonated beverage consumption. If my idiocy does catch
up with me and I break my leg by falling off the escalator, please make sure
I'm in a hospital room with an internet connection and far away from
the maternity ward.

FAILURE #20
win a prestigious award

Some people aspire to achieve greatness, to be the best and the brightest of their generation. I am not some people.

I don't have an amusing childhood anecdote about awards. I can't tell you that I've been harboring a dream of winning some highfalutin honour that would bring me the respect and riches I so desire. As a creative person, I should possess a smidge of ambition to garner some form of prestigious recognition for my work. How else will the world know how great I am? Well. I'm not, really. I am not the best at anything. I have no delusions of being the Wittiest, Prettiest, Most Perfect Thing Ever. Do I need some contest to confirm what I already know to be true?

The trouble is that in order to be considered for an award, I would first need to enter a competition. I am not competitive. Oh, I used to be when I was younger. But it was unbecoming and made me behave in most unladylike fashions. And I lost. Often. Many a board game was upended. Many a video game control thrown onto the floor. Curses everywhere. So I do my best these days to remove myself from most potentially competitive environments. I cannot resist the siren song of the shaking Boggle cube.

Even if I could muster up a healthy dose of good sportsmanship, competitions still have two deterrents: entry fees and submission guidelines. So many writing and design competitions have ridiculous entry fees. Let's see, would I rather pay $50 for the slim chance that someone will view my work and form some sort of opinion about it or buy groceries? At least food doesn't judge my work and make me feel like I've made horrible mistakes in my career choices. Maybe it's just to weed out the riff-raff and hacks, but it always feels like the organization sponsoring the competition is saying, "If you were really serious about your work, you wouldn't blink an eye at paying this entry fee. But I guess you're not a serious artist." No, I am a starving artist. Or I would be if I paid you $50.

Then there are the submission guidelines—the arbitrary criteria agreed upon by a committee which may or may not possess any relevant creative experience to draw from in setting competition requirements. After spending most of my life not quite meeting society's standards, I find that I also do not meet the criteria for these competitions. There's not much demand for Caucasian women who write plays about anthropomorphic shampoo bottles, poetry about kitchen appliances, or squiggly robots donning silly hats and sipping martinis. My work lacks the edge and emotional grit that judges are looking for. Perhaps if the shampoo bottle were used in a graphic sexually violent act, I might stand a chance as third runner-up. As it stands, I just don't tick a lot of boxes. Sure, I could create work specifically for a competition. That could also turn into a lot of spec work that never sees the light of day. And that's time that could be spent drawing robots or writing a sitcom about whimsical USB devices.

Winning is not a life goal of mine. That isn't to say that I would refuse an award if offered. On the contrary, I would snatch it up, clutch it to my nonexistent bosom and scamper off into the KatCave. Where then I would discover that, once again, my name had been misspelled. Such is the life of a Katharine.

The goal of this Katharine is to amuse people with her silliness. Every positive email or review I get from a random stranger about my book, that's my reward. Whenever I've got my little table of crafts and someone giggles at my illustrated robot in a funny hat, that does so much more for my pessimistic little soul than any foil-stamped parchment ever could. I don't make things to withstand the harsh criticism of my peers. I make things to get away from the stress of life, to create a tiny oasis of joy that someone can carry with them and gaze upon and say, "Tee hee."

things to do by age 30

1. Live alone.
2. Drink more water.
3. Watch the sunrise.
4. Take a road trip.
5. Read the news.
6. Try exotic foods.
7. Get a passport.
8. Go to the movies alone.
9. Solve a personal problem without relying on your parents.
10. Eat cake for breakfast.
11. Volunteer.
12. Wear pants that fit.
13. Move to a new town.
14. Date without pressure of commitment.
15. Spend time with people of different cultures.
16. Live with someone who isn't a blood relative.
17. Change your look at least three times.
18. Invest in a good pair of shoes.
19. Adopt two pets.
20. Sit quietly and watch the clouds roll by.
21. Learn a new skill.
22. Vote in every election.
23. Balance your work and personal life.
24. Reread the books you hated in school.
25. Organize your important documents.
26. Have an ugly cry on the bathroom floor when it all feels like too much.
27. Invest in a comfortable bed.
28. Forgive your parents.
29. Tell important people how important they are to you.
30. Stop fighting yourself.

FAILURE #21

run afoul of the law

Throughout life, we have to deal with other people's perceptions, stereotypes, and snap judgments based on our own appearances. If you had known me during the rougher moments of my life and heard that I'd been imprisoned or arrested, you wouldn't even bother to feign surprise. I have not been arrested. I have not been imprisoned. Sometimes perception is not reality.

By no means do I think myself a specimen of saintly behavior. I am a woman of loose morals and questionable ethics. My personal judgments and life decisions are deemed suspect by those with slightly narrower world views than my own. I have tested the elasticity of laws, as youth are wont to do. But my inner Jiminy Cricket always turns up and shows me right from wrong via his magic chalkboard. He's a nag, but he's kept me out of the clink.

I have two perceptions of the criminal life. One is full of romanticized notions of law-breaking and flouting authority, mobsters living the high life and attractive people pulling off complicated heists. The other is populated with unfortunate looking people who feel beaten down by The Man and have developed no discernible life skills, like the thug who rips people off just to be able to put food on his own table. Neither lifestyle holds much appeal to me.

When you straddle the poverty line (as I did), it takes very little to turn someone else's perception into your own reality. People who live in brick houses tend to not fraternize with people who live in tin boxes. I admit that living in a trailer park on the side of a major highway does seem unsavory. It reeks of cheap beer and stale cigarette smoke and rotting human dignity. You get the sense that these trailer dwellers have been on the wrong side of the law, though not entirely by their own doings. Shunned by the normals, I tried desperately to channel the cool "wrong side of the tracks" aura but my giant thick-lensed glasses betrayed me every time. And the Billy Joel songs blaring from my cheap knock-off Walkman.

These days no one mistakes me for a nogoodnik. I've long given up the wrong-side-of-the-tracks-tough-girl persona. It's difficult to be tough without coming off as borderline trashy. The dangerous denim-clad delinquent is one of those things that only men can pull off effectively. Similar to the Sexy

Professor and Cranky Curmudgeon, the Lawless Stranger is a persona that doesn't translate well across genders. Maybe it's the testosterone. Maybe it's the bushy eyebrows.

Even in my wayward awkward pre-teen years I never raised the suspicion of law enforcement officials. I haven't been accused of wrong-doing or taken downtown for questioning. Surprisingly enough, socially-awkward Caucasian girls aren't subject to much profiling. My ability to abide by laws does not prohibit me from feeling awkward when cops are in the vicinity. I never know how to behave, aside from avoiding the obvious rude behaviors. I'm not going to spit in one's face or make veiled bacon references behind their backs. But...what can I do? Is it okay to make eye contact and nod politely? Or is it proper protocol to keep your head down and avert your gaze? Am I confusing police officers with gorillas? (Note: I am not suggesting that officers and gorillas are the same. Gorillas are much scarier and more likely to go on a murderous rampage if you wink at them.) Does everybody go out of their way to avoid police interaction because they're all doing something just a little bit wrong? How is this impacting the collective self-esteems of uniformed police officers? These are questions.

I have had exactly one experience with the police. Six years ago, my boyfriend and I were trying to return home from our first Great Canadian Adventure. Hurricane Jeanne had different plans. Rather than stay holed up in a cheap Montreal motel until it was safe to fly back to Florida, we took a little side trip to New York City, where we stayed with one of his best friends. I was tired. I was bloated from all the vacation eating. I was hungover from all the fun and was ready to crawl into bed with my cats for three weeks. Instead, we went on a whirlwind sightseeing tour round NYC. The city didn't sleep and neither did we. While we were taking a roundtrip on the Staten Island Ferry, the cosmic forces decided to have a bit of a giggle. By sending over the NYPD to interrogate me for unspecified purposes. Two uniformed officers approached me while my boyfriend was on a snack hunt. What did they ask me? My brain was sounding alarms and running through all the worst-case scenarios while they were looking at my ID and asking me about the guy I was with. They escorted me over to my boyfriend, who was having a chat with two other officers, and determined neither of us were allegedly involved in criminal activity, leaving us to puzzle over the event.

Even though I have no immediate plans to flout authority and go on a crime spree, I don't believe the law is always correct. Some laws should be defied. Some should be overturned. Some just need to be gently massaged. Red buttons are meant to be pushed, boundaries redrawn, perceptions altered. But those are tasks for people who don't mind spending a night or two without internet access. If you need me, I'll be writing a letter about police etiquette to Miss Manners.

FAILURE #22
hold full-time employment

Some people believe that if you haven't worked a legitimate 9-to-5 workaday Average Joe kind of a job, you should grow up and stop wasting time on that "hobby." Those people are called "relatives." And they have not been burdened with an ever-present creative muse—a fast-talking Idea Man who can't be bothered with things like career advancement and glass ceilings and steady paycheques.

Throughout my professional life, I have been a freelancer, a temp, a part-time associate, an intern, independent contractor, a volunteer, and an hourly wage drone. That full-time steady job complete with benefits and vacation and co-workers and cubicle space has eluded me. The dream of creativity with stability remains pillow fodder. When I was at the bargaining table with the cosmic forces, haggling over the details of my adult life, some of my ambition may have been compromised. Silly me thought it would be enough to find a passion for something and learn to do it well. The cosmic mediator neglected to mention that by doing so, I was forfeiting any chance at improving my social status, income bracket, and prestige.

My parents—separately and in different stages of their respective careers—experimented with entrepreneurism with varying levels of failure. Neither of them settled into the role of small business owner or were able to wear all the hats one must when starting any sort of solo business enterprise. They were both diligent workoholics but they both overdosed on their jobs. From them, I inherited a double dose of the "be your own boss" gene. Unfortunately, the DNA was deficient in "be your own bookkeeper," "be your own efficiency expert," and "be your own sexy secretary" genes. Our common link is the belief that we'd be content being someone else's worker drones but not really wanting to answer to that someone else. At least my entrepreneur endeavors haven't ended in arson or tax blunders.

I started my career by jumping in as a freelance writer. I was a young go-getter and eager to snap up whatever assignments I could. I went. I got. I burned out on trying to keep up with researching things of which I knew nothing to write 1,500 moderately clever words every week. I hoped for a full-time writing gig that would allow me to nestle up to one broad topic. Then I had

my heart broken when one client strung me along with a job offer, only
to snatch it away without explanation. Never one to leave me stranded,
my muse popped up and introduced me to a little blue robot who took me
on a different path for a while.

I am not opposed to the idea of working for The Man. Freelancing
(and its sometimes extended droughts) is lonely work. There are no
incompetent co-workers to loathe. There are no lovely, completely competent
co-workers to befriend. There is no daily commute. There is absolutely no
reason for me to wear any of my nice, mostly business-appropriate attire.
After ten years of setting my own hours and working at my own pace, am I too
old and set in my ways to jump into a steady daytime job? Would it be a bit like
telling Peter Pan it's time to grow up? When potential employers look at my
resumé and see so much independent work, are they worried that I'll be too
independent for their office?

Today I am over 30 and the job market is dry. I live in a city full of colleges
and universities that are cranking out younger, more energetic graduates
who can be easily molded into good worker drones. As a designer,
I'm competing with 20-year-olds with flashier portfolios and 45-year-olds with
more job experience. As a writer, I'm up against everyone with a blog and
a flimsy grasp on grammar rules. Frustrations abound. My muse reports in
daily with a fresh crop of big ideas, some of which overreach my talent and
technical prowess. While I wait for the opportunity that allows me to wear
fancy pants, I am tackling my list of fancy plans and putting my muse's
more accessible ideas into action.

FAILURE #23
contract chicken pox/measles

The good news: The inoculations I received in 1985 for the four major numbered diseases were successful. The bad news: There are six numbered diseases and I caught the fifth one. Twice. There is no number six.

I was never a fit and robust child. While other kids were running around outside, shrieking and having a wholesome innocent childhood experience, I was inside trying to keep my Rainbow Brite from sleeping around with all the male toys and organizing my crayons by name, sharpness, and which colours were friends (no one ever liked Burnt Sienna). My caretakers were obsessed with keeping me "safe" and were not encouraging of any activity involving movement, sound, or my behaving like a normal child. "Sit down and shut up" was their mantra for many years. And it worked until I enrolled in grade school.

Once I was in school, my health went on a steady decline. In addition to the discovered dullness of two senses, I was a germ and fire ant magnet. My physical well-being was always in question. From the ages of six to eight, I had multiple colds, sore throats, insect bites, several bouts of Fifth virus, and a full-body allergic reaction to penicillin. My mother had failed to protect me from terrible things. My sister was pissed that I required so much attention. My baby teeth were falling out. My glasses were pink. My life was a series of maddening annoyances. I couldn't win.

I tend to be plagued with maladies that are not life-threatening but no one really knows about them. The great thing about chicken pox is everyone knows what it is, even if they haven't had it themselves. If you're a six-year-old and someone asks why you missed school, you can say, "I had chicken pox" and that someone will nod knowingly, pat you on the head, and send you along to do whatever six-year-olds do. Fifth virus manifested itself as a rash on my belly and face. I recall at least one occasion of my mother hauling me and my rash into school before the first bell to show my teacher why I'd be missing school. I was mortified as she told me to lift my shirt to display my itchy belly to Mrs. Elmore. I'm pretty sure Mrs. Elmore would've been content with whatever doctor's note I brought in on a healthier day. But maybe I'd run out of officially sanctioned sick days. Or, since fifth virus is also colorfully known as "slapped cheek disease," my mother didn't want to be accused of physically abusing me. Everyone knows psychological abuse is better because the wounds are internal and long-lasting, especially if you continue to pick at the scabs 20 years later over leftover cheesecake in motel rooms.

The closest I got to the chicken pox experience was my surprise reaction to penicillin. I developed a full-body rash while taking antibiotics to recover from a bout of strep throat. I spent a week in misery, alternating between hiding under heavy blankets to break my fever (and escape Phil Donahue's transvestite interrogations and Luke & Laura's latest misadventures) and thrashing about in discomfort. After several experiences with giant fire ant bites, I'd built up some resistance to scratching. But, man! The temptation is hard to resist. Scratching an itch is instinctual. And when it's done just right... well, there aren't many things in life that induce so much satisfaction. The friction of fingernail on skin is a sensation that is not easily matched. Benadryl and calamine lotion cannot compare to the simple scratch.

Armed with the knowledge of my actual limitations, we learned how to keep me safe without subjecting me to a life of absolute stillness. My mother arranged it so that my encounters with other children were limited to classrooms and play dates with pre-approved children. If I missed school, it was because I was in my mother's office watching *Bewitched* on my portable black and white television or sitting in the crippled children's clinic to deal with my malfunctioning ears. It would be some years before my belly was exposed again in any public setting.

As an adult, I'm not sure how likely it is that I could catch chicken pox now. It seems unlikely as I don't find myself surrounded by children very often. To be safe, I always cross to the other side of the street when passing a pack of grade schoolers. I avoid popular parks and any activity where children are in abundance. Mostly I stay inside, trying to prevent sexual promiscuity amongst my plush moose and organizing my PrismaColor markers by name, usability, and musical talent. Some habits are hard to break.

FAILURE #24

get married

Love and marriage—Frank Sinatra crooned that you can't have one without the other. Sorry, Ol' Blue Eyes, but the heterosexuals are disproving your myth —marrying without love, loving without marriage, and disparaging the entire institution. We're rebels, Frankie baby.

Before I begin, let's clarify something: "getting married" and "being married" are very different things in reality. Ladies can spend an entire year focused on the task of getting married. Little girls fantasize about getting married, they rarely fantasize about being married. Getting married is about weddings and fancy dresses and giant cakes and presents from long forgotten relatives. Being married is decidedly less glamourous. I failed to get married.

Marriage is one of those traditions that everyone is assumed to take part in. But no one really discussed it with me and asked whether it was something I'd like to do someday. My own parents had several divorces between them and 100% divorce rate. Bitterness consumed my mother after her last divorce and she soured on men altogether. To this day she cannot be convinced that men have any redeeming qualities. My poor boyfriends never stood a chance. Nobody taught me to play house or instilled in me the desire to take care of a husband/family. While other girls dreamed about being princesses and mommies, I dreamed about being a self-sufficient modern woman—a jetsettin' lady leaving an international trail of broken hearts. To be fair, no one told me about any of that either.

I didn't even think about marriage until my first serious boyfriend in high school. Sixteen sounds too young to consider the prospect of marriage. Unless you live in Alabama. Serious Boyfriend #1 and I sometimes played the game of "what would it be like if we got married." We'd get all mooneyed and imagine white picket fences and cute cottages and tricked out entertainment centers... wait, why does he get to play with all the cool electronic toys? Do we need so many game consoles? I want to play *Tetris*! Y'know, if we get a smaller television, we can buy a hot tub...Whaddya mean what's for dinner? We realized that a mutual love for *The Tick* animated series and Weird Al was not a solid foundation for lifelong partnership but did make for some short-term laughs. And we learned an important lesson in trying to make out to George Carlin's HBO specials.

Serious Boyfriend #2 entered my life before my senior year and stuck with me through my first year in university. Somewhere along the line, we got engaged. I thought it was a pretend engagement, something to pacify the parents while we spent all of our waking hours and most of our non-waking hours in each other's company. Apparently, there's some unwritten societal rule that couples can only be together for six-to-eighteen months before everyone starts nagging about wedding dates and offspring. Because I assumed the engagement was an open-ended ruse until we eventually broke up (and we *were* breaking up, right? *Right?!*), I had no intention of planning a real wedding. This wouldn't do. Everyone expected us to set a date. Serious Boyfriend #2 became Perturbed Fiance. Silly people. They thought I would plan one of those traditional weddings with flowers and frilly dresses and family. Had they met me? I grew discouraged after finding that the bride's side of the...chapel-like location would be sparse compared to the groom's side. In order to receive wedding presents from people your parents only mention in passing on the big holidays, you have to invite them to the actual wedding. And they feel obligated to show up. The whole event was becoming distasteful to me. Perturbed Fiance seemed open to the idea of elopement. So much for pretending!

As I said, I failed to get married.

Cohabitation, on the other hand, is something I can live with. Cohabitation without expectation is even better. Since Perturbed Fiance became Serious Ex-Boyfriend #2 instead of Ex-Husband #1, I have lived with two men. Once with the far-off intentions of marrying and settling down in a small town, which didn't jibe with my jetsetting lady plans. Now I cohabit with a man who is also not the marrying kind. Our mutual love for each other has kept us together for an unspecified amount of time and provided long-term giggles and guffaws. We agree that fancy parties are not necessary for us to celebrate our relationship, even if we don't agree which way to turn the spoons in the dishwasher.

Marriage is sneaky, as my boyfriend and I learned a few years ago. Apparently, in the eyes of some governments—including the one in our newly adopted country—couples who have been together an unspecified amount of time (hey, that's us!) are considered common-law spouses. So, my once Secret Boyfriend has evolved into my Common-Law Partner. Without any ado, I am, for all intents and purposes, married. I guess Sinatra was right after all. These boots are made for walkin'...wait.

FAILURE #25
visit a strip club

I'm sorry that I won't be able to titillate you with ribald tales of near encounters with professional nude dancers. In fact, to my conscious knowledge, I have had zero encounters with dancers in any state of undress. What happens in my unconscious state stays in my unconscious state. To further disappoint you, I have no fascinating stories of how I've managed to avoid nudie bars. I do have some theories, though, if you're interested.

The obvious theory as to why I have never visited a strip club is simply unavailability. Assuming, of course, that it is naked gentlemen I'd like to see wriggling about and not naked ladies. Gender inequality still reigns in the sex industry as even in the 21st century, strip clubs catering to women are rarities. In Alabama, male strip clubs must not exist at all. Surely, if there was one in the 1990s, my sexually-curious gal pals and I would've sought this out, procured fake IDs and gone on an adventure. Y'know, for research purposes." Instead we were left with the notion that if you want to see a naked boy, you just ask him to take off his clothes. Occasionally, the Chippendales tour would roll into town. My sister went to one of their shows once and returned home with a souvenir thong and a photo of a dancer. I was fascinated...until I saw the dancer's picture—a greasy orange man with a blonde mullet and sleazy grin.

Which brings me to my next theory: I do not like the same boys that other girls like. Or possibly more accurate is that I do not like the boys the sex industry expects women to like. Hairless, oiled-up beefcakes have no arousing impact on me except arousing the desire to go to Boston Market for some rotisserie chicken. While other girls may be content to swoon over men who spend more time at the gym than the library, I prefer my men a little more endowed upstairs. I prefer substance over style, brains over brawn, and wit over width. Sadly, if girls like me want to see nude clever, intelligent men we have to settle for archival photos of naked members of Monty Python on Tumblr. Or just ask our clever, intelligent boyfriends. Maybe it wouldn't be the same experience as watching a professional pelvic-gyrator because smart men don't wear shiny underpants.Everything I know about strip clubs was learned from television and movies. No one ever looks happy in a gentlemen's club. The dancers are disengaged with fixed, vacant stares. The men are creepy and lewd. It all seems like some puritanical attempt to dissuade people from visiting such places. But I'm curious to find out if strip clubs really are as depressing as the buildings seem in daylight. My mother and I took many roads trips to Florida and would see all of the We Bare All billboards dotted along I-75. I was always a little intrigued to go to the Risqué Cafe and see if it warranted all the signage. My mother would just giggle and keep driving. But imagine the kind of story I would have of my mother and I going to a strip club, seated amongst sweating truckers and shifty-eyed locals. What gems would I have from the woman who, while I was purchasing some new pants, once turned to me as the cash register rang up my trousers as 'Active Bottoms' and exclaimed "No, no!" Apparently bottoms should remain inert. Dirty jokes abound.

Surprisingly, none of my heterosexual boyfriends insisted on taking me to a nudie bar. There were discussions. Jokes were made. I never entirely rejected the idea. But we never even ventured into a strip club parking lot. Nerdy boys talk a very good game of how they only like "real girls" and are put off by silicone and latex undergarments. It's just as well they never took me. I would only mock and judge. While at a karaoke bar, I spent most of the evening mocking the graphics and font choices. Analysis of a dancer's song and costume choices does not make for sexy times.

Do we even need strip clubs anymore? Who needs to risk embarrassment at exotic dance clubs when we've got the internet? Through the magic of technology, anyone can do a Google image search for their scantily clad gender of choice and have plenty of objects to ogle without a midnight trip to the bank machine. I suppose some things must be experienced in the flesh. Will curiosity eventually get the better of me? Will I muster up the courage to experience an exotic establishment and risk being viewed as a lady pervert? Probably not.

FAILURE #26
defend myself

I have a black belt in repression. I have mastered the art of turning the other cheek. I took all of those sticks and stones and built a fortress in honor of the great comeback spirit of Nyah Nyah.

Look, I hate fighting. Confrontations require a lot of effort, what with the yelling and the maintaining the anger level to sustain the argument. I've found that it's easier to let the other person express their dismay, nod empathetically, and move on. Then I can watch television in peace. Despite years of teasing and unpleasant encounters, I am a relatively non-confrontational, cool-headed person—perhaps to a fault. I have a temper that I am uncomfortable with unleashing, so I prefer to remain disengaged from arguments, regardless of whether I am right or my own level of anger. Oh, and I never learned how to fight properly.

It's become cliché now to say I had a bad childhood. Everyone had a crummy childhood. No one was happy and everyone was misunderstood. I'll say I had an unfortunate childhood. Before I enrolled in grade school, I was a cute little kid who sat a little too close to the television and made up adorable words like "HeeHee World" for Disney World and "fayfay" for horsey. Once I entered first grade, I was suddenly the love child of Mr. Magoo and Elmer Fudd. In a perpetual state of squinting, I would have conversations with hat wacks and walk into wabbit holes. Within six months or so, we learned that I couldn't see, hear or talk vewwy well. And from that point on, everyone would accuse me of it all being an elaborate wuse, er, ruse.

My mother went into protective mode. She lobbied to get me into the special education classes, but I was not mentally-challenged (contrary to what my maternal grandmother liked to tell her friends) nor did I have a learning disability. She attached a black elastic sports strap to my delicate pink plastic glasses, so that I wouldn't lose them. She went to my teachers to explain all of the conditions for special treatment I would require in their classrooms. I didn't stand a chance.

At the time, I didn't understand that kids will look for anything to tease each other about. It's the kid way. I had no experience with real children, just the

JW-programmed kidbots and sitcom kids. So when classmates started picking
at me about my eyesight and the way I pronounced words and my noisy
corduroy pants, I took it to heart. I wasn't aware that I was supposed to point
out their flaws in an unkind manner as well. As I saw it, they were right.
These were things that were wrong with me. "But why-y-y-y?" I would whine
to my mother. "Why are they picking on me-e-e-e-e all the time?" She advised
me to ignore them. "Drive your own desk" was her favourite response
to any issue I had with other children. No one taught me to be assertive and
stand up to the bullies. All the adults said, "Tell a teacher. Go to a grown-up
if someone's being mean to you."

My approach to dealing with bullies was three-fold. My first plan of defense
was to cry. "That'll show 'em," I thought. "They'll make fun of me and I'll just
burst into tears. Then they'll feel so bad and leave me alone." If that didn't work,
I'd shout "Leave me alone!" and squint at them. When that didn't work, then
I'd go to a teacher and tell her that the brats on the playground kept kicking
rocks in my face. Ha. Ha. Ha.

The grown-ups fought my battles for me. The teachers were well aware
of both my disabilities and took care to set me out in the hall while they lectured
the whole class about picking on people with disabilities. In those moments,
I wished I'd been in the special ed class. Those kids were nice to each other.
The class was small, so the teacher could give equal attention to the students.
They held hands whenever they left the classroom. But they probably didn't
watch *Bosom Buddies,* so I still wouldn't have anyone to talk to.

My sister, armed with a scowl and good intentions, would escort me up to
my school and dare other kids to mess with me. She'd hiss empty threats at the
bully *du jour.* This usually resulted with further taunts about my being a crybaby
who needed her adult sister to defend her. There were no wabbit holes big
enough to hide me. One time, one of my bullies reported my sister and the
authorities were called in. Then it was back to my three-fold plan.

It's easy in hindsight to pull a Cyrano and rattle off fabulous witty
comebacks to childhood teases. However, it wasn't all verbal teasing. Some kids
treated me like an interactive science exhibit. Despite my glasses' strap, kids still
wanted to take my glasses to see if they were real.

"Can you really not see without your glasses?"

"Let's take her glasses and make her try to read something far away."
When it got around that I had a hearing impairment, it was all "Let me whisper
something to you. Psstpsstpsst." And "Can you read lips? What am I saying

now?" followed by silent, flaccid mouth flapping. Some kids were desperately jealous that I was getting special attention and wanted to prove I was making it all up. I just put my head down and waited for something shiny to come along and distract them. If I'd wanted special treatment, I probably would've come up with something that didn't make me look (and sound) like a total dweeb. Maybe a mysterious fainting illness that would allow me to take naps.

At the beginning of sixth grade, we managed to secure a deal through the local crippled children's clinic for me to finally get hearing aids. After years of going back to the clinic every two months for testing, they determined my hearing wasn't improving and I needed to try the devices. I was excited to be able to finally hears sounds I'd never heard. And then I got to school. After my first spelling test with my new ear jewelry—and being one of the only three kids in class to ace it—some little boy who'd never acknowledged my existence before announced to the entire class that the answers to the test had been transmitted to me via the hearing aids. Back in the box went the hearing aids. I took them out again when we moved later in the school year. It was a new school and a chance to start over. But it only brought more nasty children saying nasty things. I found that a rumour was circulating that I had aids. Back in the box went the hearing aids and back to the clinic went the box.

By the time I got to junior high, I was a pathological mess. Convinced that people were going to make fun of me no matter what, I just gave up. I stopped brushing my hair. I rarely changed clothes. People would ask me things and I would make up complicated untruths. I stopped trying at school, just exerting the minimum amount of effort to prevent outright failing. It was easier to feign disinterest in academics than to get all the teachers involved and deal with more grown-up pity in addition to the teasing. My mother and I had decided I was old enough to deal with my teachers myself and there were too many of them for her to meet with to explain that I was damaged goods. My smells and bad attitude kept everyone a safe distance away.

High school offered another chance at reinvention. I was old enough for contact lenses and could finally pretend that I was physically normal. People could tease me about my Daffy Duck sock collection instead. Ultimately, I ignored my disabilities and repressed the emotional pain instead of finding a way to embrace and fully overcome my disabilities while raising awareness. I should have found a way to be assertive and inform people about hearing loss and encourage them to be more sensitive to the issue. At the time, it was more important to me to be a (very silly) person than a cause.

Insults are like styrofoam—they might be intended for one-time use but they don't break down easily and aren't easily absorbed into the emotional landfill. I'm trying to shrink my emotional carbon footprint by limiting the amount of bile and unnecessary cruelty I release into the world. Sometimes that means I don't get to win a fight. It might mean I don't get the chance to defend myself against unfair accusations. It's okay. I've got four cheeks.

FAILURE #27
own property

When I was a kid, the attributes of a well-adjusted Grown Up seemed clear. Grown Ups were married, they had children and full-time jobs, and they owned houses. Grown Ups had the middle class comfort that was the standard to which we aspired. It wasn't the American Dream, it was the American Expectation. Even I, with my affinity for defying expectations, assumed that I would one day assimilate and become a Grown Up. Then I grew up.

Middle class comfort is as attainable a goal as becoming a fairy tale princess for those living in lower class squalor. While other little girls imagined living in prim Colonial-style houses with white picket fences, I imagined finally having my own bedroom and not sharing a bed with my mother. My only architectural concern was whether there were four walls and a door that could be properly slammed. When I did fantasize about The Future and a place for my stuff, I never considered a proper house. I had loft ambitions—exposed bricks and beams, giant windows, four walls and a door. In The Future, I was going to be an Independent City Girl living in a sexy apartment. Well, at least I got the City part down.

Just as I was not blessed with the Business Savvy gene, the Home Owner gene is also missing from my DNA. My parents were not avid home owners. My mother was a serial renter and my father had the charming habit of purchasing houses and then putting the deeds into his lady friends' name. Both parental units were terrified of having property attached to their own names, living in constant fear that everything they owned could be snatched away without warning. Whether this fear was a symptom of their divorce or of being born in the Silent Generation or just being lower class Caucasians prone to fits of general fuck-uppery, I'll never know for certain.

My mother was in the real estate research business. At the request of banks or other lending corporations, it was her job to track the history of ownership for residential properties. I spent many afternoons and summers accompanying her on adventures through the local court house, digging up relevant information on homeowners and their properties. Oh, the information that's accessible to anyone who's being paid to ask for it would have privacy advocates reeling! We flipped through thousands of files on Johnsons, Williams, and Smiths and their residential history. We learned where the Johnsons got divorced, which Williams had the most tax liens, how many times the Smiths refinanced their mortgage. I didn't wholly understand the information I was gathering, but I did enjoy the blue glow of the microfiche. Our research could turn up pages of deeds and mortgages and foreclosures just on one property. Seeing the kind of legal drama that can unfold in home buying—even without HGTV's quick cuts and tension-building edit—didn't instill great consumer confidence in the real estate industry.

I've been content as a renter. Many people make a lot of noise about how renting is just throwing money away or paying someone else's mortgage. I like renting when it means someone else is responsible for the outdoorsy bits and structural maintenance. It's nice to have someone to blame when the house breaks. Home ownership is a major purchase and a huge responsibility. One could even argue that it's bigger than marriage. Unless you're a house-flipper or just trying to get a leg up on that property ladder, the house you buy is presumably the house you'll live in for a substantial chunk of your life. So, it's not enough to fall in love with a house (unless it's portable), there's the neighbourhood to consider…the city, the country. Well, at least I got the country part down.

Things have changed since I was a kid. Expectations have shifted. Thanks to the invention of the Quarterlife Crisis, we can defer adulthood along with college loans. No one really expects new 30-year-olds to own much of anything. The middle class is not as comfortable as it was a few years ago. It looks like we need new social norms by which to measure our failures and successes. I am master of my own web domain…that counts for something, right?

FAILURE #28
perform in public

I could have been a performer but I never had the bosom. I never had the bosom to give me the confidence to go up before a live audience and amuse them with a performance. As it is, I lack the stage presence necessary to capture and retain the attentions of an audience.

For years, I worked to cultivate some kind of proficiency in the performing arts. I tried dance, music, and theatre to no avail. The absence of busty substances further eliminated a number of performance-related vocations such as Go-Go Dancer, Magician's Assistant and Sexy Mime. My dreams of writhing about silently on stage were shattered. I managed to become a writer instead.

My interest in performing was limited to narrating stuffed animal plays and playing Tape Recorder DJ. My family liked for me to sing songs in my Fuddian English style. To say I had ambitions for stage and screen would have been quite an untruth. Despite all my creativity, I am still just a frog in a box. When confronted with an audience participation bit with Beauregard (the janitor Muppet) at a live action Muppet show, I pulled my itchy skirt over my head.

At the height of the original *Dirty Dancing* craze, I had the opportunity to take dance lessons. Thank you for asking, but no, I did not have the time of my life. We were chubby little girls in leotards mastering the step ball change and *pas de bourrée* to the tune of Taylor Dane. I don't think any of us were Rockettes-bound. My mother couldn't afford the costumes for the annual recital, which was only disappointing to the sliver of ego that imagined I'd be discovered on the stage of some high school gymnasium in Alabama. The instructor choreographed the numbers for the recital and shuffled me off into a corner so I could clomp and twirl about for the duration of the class.

In junior high, we were offered the option of either taking home economics or joining the school band. I was completely uninterested in domestic matters. Independent City Girls don't worry about running a household and learning practical life lessons. If they did, chick lit novels would be much shorter. So I joined the band. The stupid school band with a stupid limit to the number of students who could be percussionists and saxophonists. Because everybody wants to be Mr. Black and every kid wants to be a drummer. I say, unhook your

minds Junior High Band Instructors. Invent a new sound for the South and
be the first all-drum-and-saxophone band in the region.
Alas, we conformed and I picked a clarinet that I named Norman. Norman and
I spent our off-hours learning television themes and making sounds that only
experimental musicians could appreciate. There were recitals that I'm sure
I was obligated play in. Clarinets generally had three parts. Two kids would be
first, four on second, and twelve on third. Guess who was on third. Norman and
I went through the motions but we weren't really invested in contributing to
"Angels We Have Heard On High" and the *Batman* motion picture theme.

Norman and I parted ways and I threw myself into my writing.
I was on track to be a Serious Journalist and dedicated myself to my high school
newspaper. With diploma in one hand and squashed dreams in the other,
I went on to university as a theatre major. My new dream was to become
a playwright. And I was...for two ghastly one-act plays...that received ghastly
one-time performances. The tech booth was visible to the audience for the
one-act I had video recorded for posterity. I can be seen in the video cringing
and wincing through most of the show, the mortification completely deafened
me to audience reaction. My acting class forced me on stage for a recital of
monologues to be performed in front of my mother and everyone else's family
(Performing for family is a bit like changing in the communal locker room.
Does it count as public"?). I performed a monologue from *Electra,* in which
I accuse my mother of murdering my father. Obviously this is not the part of the
story where I describe my newfound love of the stage and the pleasure
of interpreting text for audience enjoyment.

In my one stage performance I wasn't terribly nervous. I didn't suffer from
stage fright. I just became overly aware of the voice emanating from my mouth.
It was...wrong somehow. Four years of speech therapy and a lifetime
of television viewing rendered me without that signature Southern accent.
My voice can be accurately described as monotone Valley girl. I hadn't paid
much attention to my voice; I was preoccupied with my physical appearance.
My internal monologist sounds drastically different from the sounds that trip
and stumble out of my voice box. This voice was not an elegant one.
No audience would ever be captivated by it. My vocal chords do not produce
tones that are velvety or silky or any other audible fabric that people might want
to roll around on naked. I could have been a performer with an awful voice if I'd
had the body for it. Writers can have any sort of body or voice and it doesn't
matter at all.Except...does it matter? Video might have killed the radio star,

but what will finally kill the writer? Will it be the book tour, wherein writers are coerced to read aloud passages from their latest tome? When writers are encouraged to record podcasts of their books and articles for the non-readers, will once cherished scribes be dismissed for having a funny voice? Perhaps I can track down Norman and together we can perform interpretive squeaks of these essays, a *Peter and the Wolf* for the modern age. Yes, this will make for a very interesting Fringe show. Ribbit.

FAILURE #29
leave north america

To be a truly fascinating person, it seems, one must have come from Somewhere or gone Somewhere. Books are far more interesting when the writers have traveled to distant lands to learn important life lessons. The life lessons picked up after hours in a Best Buy parking lot, while valid and pertinent, are not so easily romanticized. Sunsets viewed from the window of TGI Friday's are not as breathtaking as when viewed from the balcony of a hotel in Greece. Or so I assume. I've never been to Greece. Or anywhere else east of the Atlantic Ocean. I am not yet a fascinating person.

I could bemoan my lack of a jetsetting lifestyle. I could whine about not having the opportunity to take class trips abroad. I could shake a fist at my mother for not getting involved in a foreign exchange student program. Instead I'll remind you (and myself) that international travel is not a given. Traveling overseas is still a privilege, a luxury afforded to those with expense accounts and independent wealth. It just seems a more tangible dream thanks to globalization, modern air travel and credit cards. It's easy to forget that some people have never ventured farther than the neighbouring town.

Vacations should be fun and relaxing. I've seen brochures with blissed out people, scantily clad and frolicking about in glee. What the vacation brochures should show are late night scrambles to find empty motel rooms on a questionable stretch of interstate and hordes of cranky American tourists queued up for theme park rides.

Family vacations were not the norm amongst the working class in Alabama. It was a big deal for the land-locked to visit the beaches in Fairhope or Gulf Shores. Extended families would load up a convoy for north Florida and squish into motel rooms, Spring Break-style. With no extended family to speak of, my mother and I were unable to put our CB radio slang to use. Through some of her work friends, my mother discovered the joy of cruising and we were soon international travelers.

I have been to the Bahamas five times. Now you're wondering why I love the Bahamas so much that I would go there five times. I don't. I haven't found anything to love about the Bahamas. No offense to the tourism board and their attempts to make their country appealing to visitors. Granted, I have not been to the ritzier parts of the islands. My experience has been limited to Nassau's Centreville, where the cruise ship passengers are dumped off and left to seek out parasailing and moped rentals. My travel companions could not be persuaded to explore the island beyond the dinky souvenir shops as we eked by the hair braiding pavilion. The desperate aggression that the islanders resort to for tourist dollars is sad and a little off-putting. I have been to the Bahamas so many times because those cruises were often cheaper and the right length of time to be trapped in the middle of open waters with my cranky family members.

As a moderately intelligent, liberal, white American, I carry some guilt over not immersing myself in some form of international culture. I still haven't learned a second language. I stuff my homemade quesadillas with pineapple and coconut. I put ketchup on my Kraft Dinner. I spend my toonies at Timmy's on iced capps and double doubles.

To make up for my lack of exposure to true ethnic diversity, I now live in a cultural mosaic. Toronto is a prime example of what would happen if Epcot's World Showcase were applied to the real world. Condensed cultures from various countries are contained to neighbourhoods throughout the city. We've got Little Italy, Greektown, Koreatown, and two Chinatowns. Americans complain about Spanish infiltrating their conversational air space. In Toronto, dozens of accents and languages filter through the air. If you don't like the language, walk five blocks and it'll be something different.

With so many countries represented in Toronto, I'm hard-pressed to find reasons to travel abroad. I suppose I'd like to see the Irish countryside in person. From what I've seen in calendars, there are lots of kitty cat faces to smoosh in Greece. But does the beauty outweigh the inconvenience of the actual traveling? Just to take a two-hour flight from Toronto to Atlanta means getting to the airport two hours in advance, thanks to terrorism and threat-level orange. I would need to stay in a foreign country at least three weeks to make up for all the stress of travel. I would also require a wealthy benefactor and lively companion to fund the trip and make sure I didn't get abducted by swarthy men in dark glasses who feast on the flesh of pale friendless ladies. Since I don't anticipate the acquisition of a wealthy benefactor in the near future, I will settle for bubble tea, saganaki, and poutine while wandering the streets of my favourite city.

FAILURE #30
be truly selfless

Is it possible to be truly selfless in the 21st century? Are you able to donate more than your wealth, to give your time and yourself to causes outside of your personal needs and desires? I'm not. I am guilty of selfish behavior and complete obliviousness to the needs of others. I walk around town plugged into my handheld entertainment device, dodging the shapeless masses walking toward me. I quickly avoid eye contact with people more disheveled than myself. Did someone fall down? I'm already half a block away.

I have a reputation amongst my closest acquaintances for being misanthropic. It is true that I detest the current state of the human race, but I didn't choose misanthropy. I didn't wake up one morning and decide it would be great fun to hate people. It was a gradual decline.

Or maybe it's hereditary.

I am third generation misanthrope. My maternal grandfather once wrote a letter to my mother encouraging her to dumb down, that people would not appreciate her for being smart and definitely wouldn't appreciate free thought. My mother passed this wisdom to me, fat lot of good it did. Thinking is a delightful hobby. Thought can lead to ideas and imagination can lead to innovation. That's how we got some of the most brilliant theories and inventions in the world. Sadly, a lot of people are afraid of thinking and thinkers. And those people will try to beat the intellectuals—physically or psychologically—into submission, shame them for being different, push them off the swings and kick rocks at their glasses.

Why should I be selfless?

What's my motivation?

I've fallen into the trap, you see. Despite all my attempts to cast off the stereotypes bestowed on me, I am still guilty of lumping All People into the category of Mean People. Once again, the minority (although, I think I'm being kind when I say "minority") of bad seeds ruin it for everyone. Not everyone is horribly insensitive and self-absorbed. Some people are kind. They are generous with their time and their love. They carve out time from their busy schedules to volunteer for causes close to their hearts. They make the effort to help those

in need. Then there are people in need. Needy People. They get the worst rap
of all. The underprivileged are painted as people to pity, dirty and helpless and
perhaps malnourished. But there are varying levels of need and people who
require assistance aren't always looking for a free ride. Sometimes they just
need a jump.

When I needed routine check ups for my hearing impairment, the best
we could afford was the local crippled children's clinic. Back then, all the
disabilities were lumped together. There we were in the waiting room, me with
my little hearing loss and toddlers with cerebral palsy and all the disabilities
in between. As far as the government was concerned, we were all crippled.
I sat in the waiting room and watched the other kids. Most times, I was the
healthiest looking in the bunch. Some of these children would need assistance
for life. They probably didn't intend to grow up into Independent City Girls.
Did I pursue independence more fiercely in their honour? No. I scurried as far
away as possible because I didn't want to be a cause. I didn't want to be crippled.
I didn't want to be—as my mother so lovingly called me—the next Helen Keller.

If I were a better person, I would turn my failures into opportunities.
I'd look for ways to contribute to society, filling in niches and luring fellow
misanthropes from their caves. I could organize a field trip to a strip club
for childfree non-drivers or an overnight camp for friendless introverts.
The possibilities are limitless. The possibilities require strength and dedication
I don't yet possess. It's still easier to avoid human interaction than to invest
myself and risk further rejection and remorse.

Is it possible for me to be truly selfless in the 21st century?
I don't know. I'll try.

what, only 30?!

Oh, gentle reader, you are hilarious! Of course there are more than 30. I am a maladjusted, socially-awkward girl-lady with no sense of how to behave in polite society. To publish all my myriad failures in one tome would surely overwhelm and frighten you. To attempt to write about every single thing I've sucked at or avoided is such a debilitating notion that it's best not to dwell. But since you've inquired, I've collected up more life experiences that have eluded me. Maybe you don't see these as failures. Maybe you have also failed at or not attempted these things. Maybe you've done it all. If you have done it all (and succeeded), please email me with your tips and secrets. Alternatively, if you'd like to give me my own television reality show in which I hilariously attempt to cross items off the list, please contact my personal manager immediately.

More items at which I have failed:
Learn to swim
Straighten teeth
Walk in high heels
Apply fancy make up
Fix relationship with family
Properly use power tools
Read and follow an instruction manual
Sit in a treehouse
Stay the whole night at a sleepover
Sing
Volunteer for charity
Memorize famous quotations
Use a sewing machine
Dabble in homosexuality
Join a rock band
Crowd surf in a mosh pit
Learn to skate (roller or ice)
Give up meat
Ride a horse
Hitch hike

Excel in chosen profession(s)
Get a tattoo or exotic piercing
Hail a taxi
Read all the great classical literature
Keep cat hair off any item of clothing
Watch the Star Wars movies
Protest for a worthy cause
Learn all the words to my national anthem(s)
Visit Graceland
Travel cross-continent on a train
Watch a movie at a drive-in
Master a musical instrument
Become a ventriloquist
Tell a joke properly
See (or name) the Seven Wonders of the World
Built a sand castle
Shoplift
Ride in a limosine
Pursue a celebrity for autograph/photo op
Throw someone a surprise party
Defrost a refrigerator
Draw a straight line
Own a gun
Climb a tree
Been to a farm
Set something on fire
Serve on a jury
Testify in court
Commit suicide
Dream of winning the lottery
Win the lottery
Aspire to pursue a noble cause
Empathize
Participate in a Boggle tournament
Make peace with being a failure

how to be a failure

1. Judge yourself by someone else's arbitrarily determined standards.
2. Allow others to ridicule you for your own personally determined standards.
3. Apply deadlines to life goals but depending on Fate to intervene in helping you meet those goals.
4. Give up on lifelong dream because your big break didn't come before you reached a milestone birthday.
5. Believe that owning a house or having a baby means you're officially grown up. More responsibility does not automatically result in instant maturity.

FAILURE BINGO

Drive a car	Master the art of small talk	Ride a bicycle	Procreate	Stick to fitness regimen
Join organized religion	Keep a best friend	Join team sports	Attend sleepaway camp	Exercise Patience
Move to NYC	Master nice penmanship	Learn a second language	Develop drug addiction	Ride a roller coaster
Stay in hospital	Win an award	Run afoul of the law	Hold full-time employment	Get married
Visit a strip club	Defend myself	Own property	Perform in public	Be truly selfless

How many things have you failed to do before turning 30?

about katharine!

Katharine is the author of *Slantindicular: Stores Among Other Things*,
The Curable Romantic: Advice for the Romance-Impaired, the best-selling
30 Failures by Age 30, and the author-illustrator of *BORIS! Robot of Leisure*.
Katharine is also an artist and graphic designer specializing in low-brow pop art
inspired by 20th century popular culture. Katharine's paintings, part of
her Robot of Leisure series, have been exhibited in galleries and public spaces
across North America. View more of her work at thatkatharine.com.

www.ingramcontent.com/pod-product-compliance
Lightning Source LLC
Chambersburg PA
CBHW071457030726

47593CB00003B/1042